Silver at Williamsburg:
Drinking Vessels

Silver at Williamsburg:
Drinking Vessels

by John A. Hyman

The Colonial Williamsburg Foundation
Williamsburg, Virginia

The Colonial Williamsburg Foundation
Williamsburg, Virginia

© 1994 by The Colonial Williamsburg Foundation

Library of Congress Cataloging-in-Publication Data

Hyman, John A.
    Silver at Williamsburg : drinking vessels / by John A. Hyman.
       p.   cm. — (Wallace Gallery decorative arts publications)
    Includes bibliographical references and index.
    ISBN 0-87935-125-X
    1. Silver drinking vessels—Great Britain—Catalogs. 2. Silver
drinking vessels—Catalogs. 3. Silver drinking vessels—Virginia—
Williamsburg—Catalogs. 4. Colonial Williamsburg Foundation—
Catalogs. I. Title. II. Series: Wallace Gallery decorative arts
publication.
NK7143.H96 1994
739.2'383—dc20   93-46616
                                                            CIP

Book design: Vernon Wooten

Photography: Hans Lorenz and Craig McDougal

Williamsburg Decorative Arts Series
Graham Hood, *Editor*

British Delft at Williamsburg
by John C. Austin

Chelsea Porcelain at Williamsburg
by John C. Austin

English and Oriental Carpets at Williamsburg
by Mildred B. Lanier

English Silver at Williamsburg
by John D. Davis

Furnishing Williamsburg's Historic Buildings
by Jan Kirsten Gilliam and Betty Crowe Leviner

The Governor's Palace in Williamsburg: A Cultural Study
by Graham Hood

New England Furniture at Williamsburg
by Barry A. Greenlaw

Rebellion and Reconciliation: Satirical Prints on the Revolution at Williamsburg
by Joan D. Dolmetsch

The Williamsburg Collection of Antique Furnishings

Wallace Gallery Decorative Arts Publications

Eighteenth-Century Clothing at Williamsburg
by Linda Baumgarten

English Slip-Decorated Earthenware at Williamsburg
by Leslie B. Grigsby

Silver at Williamsburg: Drinking Vessels
by John A. Hyman

Tools: Working Wood in Eighteenth-Century America
by James M. Gaynor and Nancy L. Hagedorn

Worcester Porcelain in the Colonial Williamsburg Collection
by Samuel M. Clarke

Contents

Foreword

Great collections, like human beings and their knowledge of the past, should continue to grow. This development can be in quantity, in quality through refinement, or in a greatly enhanced appreciation of the inherent virtues and meanings of the objects themselves. In the case of Colonial Williamsburg's collection of British silver, it is a combination of all three. An added and most pleasurable dimension of this growth has been the impact of the existing collection, and of the published work and great expertise of the curator, on the collecting impulses, the knowledge, and the percipience of a generous friend and donor.

We are deeply grateful to John A. Hyman for bringing, in his retirement, a most unusual and finely honed group of early British silver domestic objects to Colonial Williamsburg and for seeking with tireless energy to augment the already strong collections here. With ambition and élan, John further wrote this book, hoping to infect others with the same love of these brilliant, charming, evocative things as he has. His ulterior motive is to broaden and deepen the appeal that Colonial Williamsburg holds for so many.

In later pages, John has acknowledged the assistance he received from many talented staff members in the production of this book. We second those thanks and, to John D. Davis, long our curator of metals, we add a generous measure of our own.

Graham Hood
Vice President, Collections and Museums
Carlisle H. Humelsine Curator

Introduction

Colonial Williamsburg's extensive collection of silver drinking vessels is the legacy of three distinct sensibilities and reflects different philosophies of collecting over six decades. The earliest accessions were made under the auspices of John D. Rockefeller, Jr., who authorized the purchase of many of the grandest and rarest silver objects in Williamsburg's treasury. These pieces reflect his vision of Williamsburg as a repository for the most important and magnificent objects obtainable.

Additions from 1950 to the present were made under chief curators John Graham and Graham Hood. Both were keenly aware of Williamsburg's primary educational mission: to re-create the life of the colonial period by joining artifacts and buildings in an accurate presentation of eighteenth-century Williamsburg. From time to time, they have also acquired outstanding examples particularly suited to a museum collection; those are now housed in the DeWitt Wallace Decorative Arts Gallery, where they can be viewed and studied in a museum setting.

John Davis, curator of metalwork for more than a quarter-century, has been responsible for locating and recommending the acquisition of silver items ranging from the sophisticated wares of a royal governor to the single vessel cherished by a jailer as well as appropriate fittings for the taverns, the homes of artisans, merchants, and planters, and trade sites open for exhibition in the Historic Area,

all in addition to the brilliant objects on view in the Masterworks and silver study galleries in the Wallace Gallery. Such diversity is unmatched in conventional museum collections.

A substantial body of material consists of a specialized study collection assembled by a friend of the Foundation specifically to enlarge Colonial Williamsburg's holdings. One part of this study collection appears in this volume.

Thus, most unusually, three attitudes are evident in this collection. The first focused on important, rare, and significant objects, each for its own sake. The second concentrated on objects expressive of life in eighteenth-century Williamsburg. The third illustrates changes in social customs in the larger world of Great Britain and her colonies.

Two curatorial consistencies unify these groups. First is an emphasis on quality and integrity, whether the object is a towering candelabrum or a simple skewer. Second is a scrupulous regard for each object's purpose and function, coupled with respect for historic accuracy.

These objects all relate to one another, they inform on one another. Together they compose a remarkable continuum that cuts across the social, geographic, and political differences within the British Empire during the seventeenth and eighteenth centuries.

It is remarkable that three such different approaches to collecting fuse coherently, both aesthetically and intellectually. Though limited to the single topic of drinking vessels, this volume proves that such diverse viewpoints, even across the long passage of time, can coalesce into a distinctive and representative collection, suitable both for study and for simple pleasure and consistent in quality, aesthetics, and historical value.

Financial and temporal obstacles often limit opportunity, exploration, and understanding in collecting as well as publishing. John Davis's fine, intellectually rigorous catalog, *English Silver at Williamsburg* (1976), was incomplete almost as soon as it reached the public because acquisitions and learning had expanded, and continue to expand, the matrix in which objects are interpreted and understood. Then there is the most painful limitation of all: objects that are appropriate for filling out a collection often become available when there is a lack of money to obtain them.

The present catalog is incomplete for another reason: there is not enough space available for the marvelous Lowry Dale Kirby Collection of old Sheffield plate. The core of Williamsburg's great holdings in that specialized field, the Kirby Collection has been augmented by gifts from Mr. and Mrs. Oliver F. Ramsey and others. These gifts require a separate catalog to be shown in all their glory.

This catalog has been produced for the interested layperson and collector. The key is Hans Lorenz's superb photography, which reveals the beauty of these objects to the fullest. The text is intended as a supplement to his illustrations, providing essential information for understanding and enjoying each object. Despite its seeming simplicity, the text attempts to be both complete and compatible with current scholarly developments.

In the belief that continuity is important for intelligent reading, material that does not speed the basic tale has been relegated to the comments that follow each entry. A list of the books used in the preparation of this catalog has also been provided so that the interested reader can augment this material. Works that appear in this list have been given short titles in the text.

Much of the credit for this catalog does not lie with the author. Graham Hood approved it and has been generous with suggestions. John Davis has been an inexhaustible source of ideas and information, freely and modestly offered and always in the gentlest manner imaginable; his contribution has been the most significant of all.

I cannot adequately express my appreciation to Hans Lorenz, Colonial Williamsburg's museum photographer, and Craig McDougal, his assistant. They are rare in their understanding of our objects. Laurie Suber has shepherded the photography from lens to final form. Susan Shames has an awareness of source material second to none. Jan Gilliam has been generous with her knowledge of period dining and drinking customs. Betty Leviner who, as curator of exhibition buildings, understands the perils of authorship, has kept our marriage on course over what must have seemed like ages, despite my beady-eyed focus on acquisitions, research, organization, writing, and rewriting. And I have had the privilege of working with a group of bright, knowledgeable, friendly, and supportive people of whom I have grown extremely fond.

1

COVERED CUP BY THE HOUND SEJANT MAKER

The Hound Sejant Maker
London, 1649/50

Fully marked beneath base
Silver gilt
H. inc. cover 8"; H. of body 5"; Diam. at rim 4½"
Wgt. 28 oz. 17 dwt.

Formerly in the collections of Sir George Buller, Sir Samuel
   Montagu (Lord Swaythling), and William Randolph
   Hearst, 1938-32

This unknown smith is identified only by his mark, a seated (in heraldic terms, sejant) hound, but in the breadth of his vision, the certainty of his hand, and his versatility, he is the unquestioned English master of the period between 1645 and 1670. At a time when drinking vessels were customarily round, this superb twelve-sided cup must have been a radical innovation. The next recorded example of this shape is also by the Hound Sejant Maker and dates to two years later. There are three other examples, one as late as 1661. None of the other pieces has quite the presence of this example, which is as imposing as any covered cup, regardless of design and despite a total height of only eight inches; its body planes reach skyward; the cover carries higher. The handles and tucked-in foot emphasize the thrust of the form.

In *Caroline Silver*, Charles Oman shows the full range of the Hound Sejant Maker's work, including this cup, a set of dram cups, two larger cups, and a pair of towering flagons (pls. 8, 20B, 9A–9B, 31A–31B). This extraordinary range attests to his ability to adjust to diverse styles with technical mastery and a sense of the aesthetic requirements of each one. Also illustrated with additional references in Davis, *English Silver at Williamsburg* (pp. 54–56).

No. 1. Covered cup by the Hound Sejant Maker.

Lomax identifies the five known pieces (by four different smiths) in this style (*British Silver at Temple Newsam*, p. 52). What does their existence say about the shape's rarity? Though only five examples in this complex and important style survive, the fact that they were made by four different smiths suggests that this may have been a popular—or at least a desirable—design. Why otherwise would a number of makers tackle what must have been a daunting project?

2

LARGE COMMONWEALTH COVERED CUP

Unidentified mark of "AF"
London, 1655/56

Fully marked atop cover and on body at rim
Later engraved arms (ca. 1710) of Tindal of Dickelburgh, County Norfolk
H. inc. cover 7¼"; H. of body 6¼"; Diam. at rim 5"
Wgt. 41 oz. 3 dwt.

Formerly in the collections of Sir Samuel Montagu (Lord Swaythling) and William Randolph Hearst, 1938-31

In its broad stance, muscular, no-nonsense body, flat cover, and forceful, complex caryatid handles, this dramatic cup resembles nothing less than Hans Holbein the Younger's challenging portrait of Henry VIII, an icon of English art.

In terms of aesthetic satisfaction, this standing cup is more memorable than either tankards or flagons of similar design: it is visually unimpaired

No. 2. Large Commonwealth covered cup.

by the thumbpiece rolling over the cover that hollow-handled tankards require structurally. It stands above the crowd, its character unquestioned, strongly masculine and assured.

This shape is seen primarily on tankards and on taller flagons but seldom on covered cups. Only four like this one are known; all are by this same maker. Like the preceding cup, this one is included in Charles Oman's *Caroline Silver;* he also shows a decorated tankard dated 1655/56 and a flagon dated 1675/76, both based on this same design (pl. 13A). Also illustrated with additional references in Davis, *English Silver at Williamsburg* (pp. 56–58).

3
MANWARING COVERED CUP

**Arthur Manwaring
London, 1657/58**

Fully marked beneath cover and base
Contemporary engraved arms of Deighton of Hostow,
    County Lincoln, on body; crest on face of cover
H. inc. cover 5⅞"; H. of body 4"; Diam. at rim 5¼"
Wgt. 22 oz. 13 dwt.

Formerly in the collection of Mrs. Rockefeller McCormick,
    John A. Hyman Collection, 1987-831

Examples from this master's hand are included in most reference books on silver. He is closely identified with this type of repetitive, abstract patterning borrowed from Continental design, which coexisted with the repeated roundels seen on numbers 6 and 7, but this decorative treatment may

No. 3. Manwaring covered cup.

represent a more sophisticated level of the taste of the period. At the least, it embodied the more highly developed technical skills that Charles Oman has acknowledged: "Manwaring's work is notable for its fine embossing" (*Caroline Silver*, p. 31).

This cup is a typical example of vessels of this type, which are consistent in size, shape, and ornament. Many were furnished with large footed stands, most of which have gone separate ways.

The wonderful handles share a common European origin with those seen on the two preceding pieces. Such handles were transplanted to England by Dutch émigré smiths, whose pattern books included fantastic elements borrowed from the Renaissance. As with other Continental conventions, this handle type was made less complex and more direct to suit English taste (see nos. 19–21).

This cup appears in Brett, *Sotheby's Directory of Silver*, along with three others of similar design and a basin and three footed stands, all by Manwaring (pp. 126–127). It is illustrated in the American Art Association's 1934 sale catalog of the McCormick estate (where it is attributed to the goldsmith Andrew Moore) with this comment: "The exceptional rarity of English silver of the Commonwealth period is attributable to the religious fanaticism in evidence at that time, when a tremendous amount of church and other silver plate was deliberately destroyed or melted down as too worldly to suit the puritanical taste of the zealots who, for a time, controlled England. Added to this situation was the impecunious condition to which many families were reduced by civil war." The cup was exhibited at the Art Institute of Chicago in 1928 and also illustrated in Sotheby's New York sale catalog of April 20–23, 1983.

No. 4. Arcaded bowl by "IG."

4–5
TWO ARCADED BOWLS

4. Unidentified mark of "IG" over a covered cup
London, 1638/39

Fully marked beneath bowl
H. 1⁵⁄₁₆"; Diam. 3¾"; L. inc. handles 5"
Wgt. 2 oz. 18 dwt.

John A. Hyman Collection, 1988-474

5. Maker's mark badly struck; ascribed to William Maddox
London, 1638/39

Fully marked at rim
Lion passant beneath foot; later scratched inventory (?) numbers 13891/500090
H. 1⁹⁄₁₆"; Diam. at rim 3¼"; L. inc. handles 4¾"
Wgt. 2 oz. 6 dwt.

John A. Hyman Collection, 1993-8

These bowls are so named because their bodies are appreciably broader than they are tall. In use, however, they may have served the same purpose as footed wine cups (see nos. 11–13).

Regardless of shape, small silver vessels from the early seventeenth century are rare; few have survived and even fewer are so little marked by wear as these. The bowls pictured here accurately reflect their time, with crude handles and a type of punched, arcaded decoration that anticipates the more polished roundel patterns seen on numbers 6 and 7.

Comparing the two, the footed bowl seems the more graceful, more delicate and subtly aware of sophisticated design, especially the flat cast handles, whose profiles show their indebtedness to the large, flashy caryatid handles seen on more important pieces. This bowl also seems more compatible with later examples both in its design and its trumpet foot (of which this is a very early example), seen usually on mid-century wine cups (see nos. 11–13) as well as on the small two-handled London cup of 1656/57 (no. 7).

The footed bowl does not detract from the "IG" example in any way, however. The "IG" bowl may appear heavier-handed and more primitive and direct, but it conveys an innate strength that is rare in such a small vessel.

These vessels come from a culture that is foreign to us. What do we know about their use? The silver dealer Brand Inglis theorizes that they may have been used for the strong brandies derived from the final pressing of French grapes, known today as marc or grappa (conversation, London, June 17, 1992). If so, it is possible that the slightly later variations we call wine cups may have been misnamed over time and were used for beverages stronger than wine. Inasmuch as we usually drink wine

out of much larger vessels, perhaps marc, grappa, or eau-de-vie were more popular in the seventeenth century than they are today.

The "IG" bowl is illustrated in Christie's London sale catalog of October 19, 1988. A comparable bowl, dated 1642/43, is shown in Oman, *Caroline Silver* (pl. 21B). Wark, *British Silver in the Huntington Collection*, illustrates two small trumpet-footed cups, but they seem to lack the integration of shape and decoration that characterize this example (pp. 9–10).

Detail of no. 4. These small drinking vessels present unexpected vistas: a rose window, perhaps, or a cloister whose arcaded passages look out on a fountain surrounded by a carousel of plants; perhaps a wonderful, multipetaled flower in fullest bloom.

No. 5. Arcaded bowl ascribed to William Maddox.

5

TWO CUPS WITH CHASED ROUNDELS

6. Richard Neale
London, 1655/56

Fully marked at rim
Contemporary scratch-engraved initials "B C H" at rim;
  later scratch-engraved initials "I H" and date "1709" at
  rim
H. 2⅞"; Diam. at rim 4½"
Wgt. 6 oz. 17 dwt.

John A. Hyman Collection, 1990-252

7. Unidentified mark of "SA" in monogram
London, 1656/57

Fully marked at rim
Contemporary scratch-engraved initials "E A" at rim
H. 1¾"; Diam. at rim 2½"
Wgt. 1 oz. 13 dwt.

John A. Hyman Collection, 1988-184

No. 6. Cup with chased roundels by Richard Neale (left). No. 7. Cup with chased roundels by "SA" (right).

These two cups, so different in size, represent one of the rarer types of decoration surviving from the mid-seventeenth century. These designs, created by a ring of roundels with alternately matted and smooth fields, relate to the circles and ovals found on English provincial oak furniture of the period. These examples are characteristic of this style.

There is one other known example of the smaller cup, but it lacks a foot. The existence of sixteen cups in the larger size, all dating from 1650 to 1660, can be verified. The survival of such a large number may indicate that this was a popular pattern during the Commonwealth. Unlike other large cups of this period, this type seldom has a cover. There are only two recorded covered examples. One, in the Elizabeth Miles Collection at the Wadsworth Athenae-um in Hartford, Connecticut, is illustrated in the collection's catalog (Miles, *English Silver*, p. 30). The other is illustrated in plate XII of Sassoon, *Loan Exhibition of Old English Plate*, but its whereabouts are unknown.

In 1655/56, Richard Neale made another, virtually identical cup that is now in the collection of the Sterling and Francine Clark Art Institute, Williamstown, Massachusetts.

The large cup is illustrated in Christie's London sale catalogs of February 14, 1912, and May 5, 1937, and in Sotheby's London sale catalog of November 14, 1963. The bewitching smaller cup is illustrated in Sotheby's London sale catalog of November 20, 1980.

Detail of no. 6.

8–10
THREE BALUSTER WINE CUPS

8. Unidentified mark of "TM"
London, 1667/68

Fully marked at rim; lion passant beneath base
Contemporary engraved arms of Southcott of Southcott,
    County Devon, quartering M'Beath or Morden, County
    Worcester, and two sets of initials, "H*B*D" and
    "**/*RLM*/*16M87*/**"
H. 5⅞"; Diam. at rim 3½"
Wgt. 8 oz. 13 dwt.

Formerly in the collection of William Randolph Hearst,
    1938-25

9. William Rainbow
London, ca. 1630

Rainbow's mark on bowl
Contemporary engraved initials "M H" beneath foot
H. 2¾"; Diam. at rim 1½"
Wgt. 1 oz. 3 dwt.

John A. Hyman Collection, 1992-48

10. Unidentified mark of "TC" conjoined
London, 1641/42

Fully marked at rim; lion passant beneath base
Contemporary pounced initials "*O*H*/*A*" at rim
H. 6⁷⁄₁₆"; Diam. at rim 3¾"
Wgt. 9 oz. 10 dwt.

Formerly in the collections of Lady Currie and Dr. Wilfred
    Harris, 1954-587

    English silver forms exist at several levels,
including popular and useful or ceremonial and
formal. The wine cup, sometimes known as a goblet, is a case in point. The footed examples (see nos.
11–13) are lighthearted, small-scaled, and pleasurable. Their bodies and feet are made of thin sheet
metal that is easy to work and inexpensive. Their

No. 8. Baluster wine cup by "TM" (left). No. 9. Baluster wine cup
by William Rainbow (center). No. 10. Baluster wine cup by "TC"
(right).

decoration is a matter of immediate style, fitting middle-class taste.

In contrast, these baluster wine cups are serious and stentorian, following a traditional (rather than stylish) form. The bowls are solid, and the cast balusters and spread feet required more precision as well as substantially more metal. A large wine cup may have been a household's most important piece of silver. It was placed before the master of the house, who either drank exclusively from it or, after drinking, shared it with others at his table.

As an indication of their importance, baluster wine cups were among the tallest silver vessels of their time, some standing as high as nine or ten inches. A very small example, such as this exquisitely proportioned cup by the aptly named William Rainbow, is a rare treasure. Sensitively fitted with the slim tapered baluster popular as early as the first decade of the century, it bears only two initials and must have been someone's personal drinking vessel, a real source of pride to its owner, to have been so carefully maintained. Had it been commissioned to honor a special occasion or to serve as the psychological focal point of an individual or family, it would have been pounced or engraved with three initials in a triangle (a convention seen on the larger examples), the upper letter for the family name, the lower two for the given names of the husband and wife.

The two larger cups are illustrated with additional references in Davis, *English Silver at Williamsburg* (pp. 53–54). Houart illustrates an example similar to the Rainbow in size and shape that he dates circa 1630 (*Miniature Silver Toys*, pl. 188). A very early full-sized example with this baluster stem is dated 1585 and illustrated in Finlay, *Scottish Gold and Silver Work* (pl. 23). A fine cross-section of this important form can be seen in Oman, *English Silversmith's Work* (figs. 39–40, 47, 49).

THREE FOOTED WINE CUPS

11. Gilbert Shepherd
London, 1655/56

Fully marked at rim; lion passant under foot
H. 3¼"; Diam. at rim 2⅝"
Wgt. 2 oz. 14 dwt.

John A. Hyman Collection, 1991-454

12. Unidentified mark of "HN" above a bird with an olive branch
London, 1656/57

Fully marked at rim; lion passant under foot
Scratch-engraved initial "*E*" at rim
H. 2¾"; Diam. at rim 2¼"
Wgt. 1 oz. 9 dwt.

John A. Hyman Collection, 1990-62

This type of trumpet-footed wine cup was popular during the Commonwealth period. Like that of saucers (see nos. 14–18), this is a circumscribed form with a limited number of variations: size (roughly three to five inches tall), bowl shape (round or lobed), and decoration (architectural or foliate). In fact, these cups resemble infolded saucers. They even have decorated bottoms similar to a saucer's central boss. The trumpet foot, sometimes plain, sometimes textured with matting or paneled to match the bowl, is a constant element, and the chased and punched designs strongly resemble each other.

Cups of this sort are usually lightweight and perfunctorily decorated, but they are delightfully naive. Each is charming in its own way, unlike the more conventional, formal standing cups of the period (see nos. 8–10).

The Colonial Williamsburg silversmith Markham Frankel feels that the cups, mugs, and bowls of this period are especially delightful because their chased patterns can be enjoyed equally from the

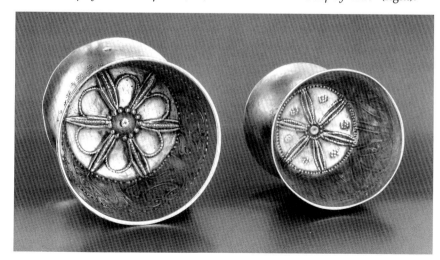

No. 11. Footed wine cup by Gilbert Shepherd (left). No. 12. Footed wine cup by "HN" (right).

Detail of nos. 11 and 12.

interior and exterior—the drinker sees the designs right through his or her beverage. This characteristic may have resulted more from technique than intent (except perhaps on the bottom, as some vessels had plain bottoms), but what an agreeable result. Here, decoration is more than exhibitionism to be appreciated by someone other than the user.

Gilbert Shepherd, one of the more prolific smiths of the Commonwealth period, made many footed wine cups. The one shown here is a particularly nice example due to the complexity of its design, which combines stylized tulips, artfully matted arcading, and what looks like an undernourished starfish (actually a stylized rosette) on the bottom.

The smaller example is illustrated in Christie's London sale catalog of July 12, 1989; the Shepherd cup is in Christie's London sale catalog of July 10, 1991. Other Shepherd wine cups are found in Brett, *Sotheby's Directory of Silver* (p. 126), and Clayton, *Christie's Pictorial History* (p. 52).

13. Andrew Gregory
Dublin, 1680/81

Gregory's mark, harp crowned, and date letter at rim of
    bowl; harp crowned beneath foot
Contemporary engraved arms possibly of Langdale,
    County York, or of Cruse, County Devon, on one side of
    bowl; contemporary engraved crucifixion scene on the
    other; contemporary engraved "D" atop foot
Round paper label with a handwritten black letter "C"
    (date letter of 1680/81) below "Irish" and above
    "1680/1" beneath foot
H. 4¾"; Diam. at rim 3¹⁄₁₆"
Wgt. 5 oz. 11 dwt.

John A. Hyman Collection, 1992-7

Despite its resemblance to the trumpet-footed wine cup popular two decades earlier, this simple, straightforward vessel was probably a sacramental chalice used by recusant Catholics, that is, those who practiced their faith in secret (the Catholic church was banned) and did not attend Church of England services. The design of the cup is based on the need to conceal the vessel. The foot unscrews and inverts to fit within the body, with the spreading foot serving as a cover. A screw-mount with its male member projecting from the bottom of the

No. 13. Footed wine cup by Andrew Gregory.

bowl, a common construction on Irish stands of the period, fastens together the foot and the body.

Few sacramental vessels bear identifying armorials, which imply secular use, but this armorial may have been employed to conceal the vessel's true nature. Alternatively, the cup may have been converted from secular to religious use shortly after it was made.

Small Irish drinking vessels of this period are especially rare; there seems to be no other surviving example similar to this one. Conventional sacramental vessels are more elaborate and follow a highly formalized design with a large knop and elaborate foot—see the example in Davis, *Genius of Irish Silver* (p. 5).

The signs of use at the rim and foot should be expected because this cup is minimally made and lacks strengthening at those wear points. Nevertheless, it is in good condition: color and texture are splendid and consistent for both foot and body, the marks are clear, and the engraved armorial and crucifixion scene are crisp.

Illustrated in Sotheby's London sale catalog of November 4, 1990.

Detail of no. 13.

14–18
FIVE SAUCERS

14. William Maddox
London, 1634/35

Fully marked at rim
Contemporary initials "TG/*/MS" within central shield
H. ¾"; Diam. at rim 5½"; L. over handles 7⁹⁄₁₆"
Wgt. 3 oz. 5 dwt.

John A. Hyman Collection, 1989-49

15. Unidentified mark of "IH" beneath a mullet
London, 1649/50

Fully marked at rim
Later pounced initials "16 RI 87" within central boss
H. 1¼"; Diam. at rim 6¾"; L. over handles 9¼"
Wgt. 6 oz. 1 dwt.

John A. Hyman Collection, 1991-456

16. Unmarked
Probably London, ca. 1640

H. ¼"; Diam. at rim 1⅝"; L. over handles 2⅜"
Wgt. 5 dwt.

John A. Hyman Collection, 1989-46

17. Unidentified mark of "IM" in oval
London, 1640/41

Fully marked at rim
Contemporary initials "MC/MG 1640" within central boss
H. ¾"; Diam. at rim 5½"; L. over handles 7¾"
Wgt. 3 oz. 10 dwt.

Formerly in the collection of Mrs. C. J. Devine, Sr., John A. Hyman Collection, 1989-47

18. Unidentified mark of "RD" in shield
London, 1671/72

Fully marked at rim
H. ¾"; Diam. at rim 5½"; L. over handles 7¾"
Wgt. 3 oz. 10 dwt.

Formerly in the collection of Mrs. C. J. Devine, Sr., John A. Hyman Collection, 1989-48

Clockwise from top: No. 14. Saucer by William Maddox. No. 15. Saucer by "IH." No. 16. Unmarked saucer. No. 17. Saucer by "IM." No. 18. Saucer by "RD."

Saucers such as these did not accompany cups in the seventeenth century, but were used for serving the pungent sauces that formed an important part of the cuisine of the period. They are included in a book on drinking vessels because they highlight important design concepts employed on other forms of the period, particularly the trumpet-footed wine cup (see nos. 11–13). First, the bowls are either round or lobed. Second, the designs are created around a central point, either the boss of the saucer or the decoration in the bottom of the wine cup. Third, the bodies are divided into regular segments, defined by outline chasing or punched beadwork, that enclose repetitive patterns borrowed mostly from the Dutch. If you mentally unfold a wine cup and visualize it laid flat, you can see how it resembles a saucer. It is amazing that wine cups and saucers are available in such variety, considering the limited number of abstract, naturalistic patterns employed on them.

Saucers are flashy and flimsy. They may be crudely made, but they are tightly organized in symmetrical patterns that are pleasingly, strangely familiar because they are universal. The standardized shell handle defines the saucer the way the trumpet foot defines the wine cup.

There are several alternative explanations for their use. First, they may have been part of large services, employed specifically by servants preparing and serving sauces to a diner. Second, being cheaply made and primitive in design, they may have been used by lower-gentry families to serve sweetmeats at dessert. Third, though a secular form, they may have been employed as patens at communion.

These five examples span the entire period during which saucers were popular (their popularity peaked during the 1630s). They illustrate the variety possible using a limited number of abstract,

naturalistic patterns borrowed from the Dutch and only two bowl variations, round or lobed. Both the large and the unusually small saucer are rare because of their size. Few saucers are more than six inches in diameter. Miniature saucers are rarer still, far rarer than miniature bowls or cups, a pity because they are so appealing. Who knows how anything so small, so easily misplaced, so perishable has survived for nearly four centuries.

Philippa Glanville writes, "Miniatures were often regarded not simply as playthings but as the means to train children in their future roles: girls were given fashionably dressed dolls, chairs and tables and miniature tableware so that they could practice domestic rituals." She also illustrates a William Maddox saucer of 1633/34 almost identical to the one shown here. Designs were probably formulaic with each maker repeating his own familiar decorative pattern. In analyzing the form, she notes, "These saucers are a symptom of the shift towards a more recognisably modern meal structure and method of food presentation, a process which by the end of the century had banished saucers in favour of sauceboats." (*Silver in Tudor and Early Stuart England*, pp. 441, 449, 223).

Both the "IM" and "RD" saucers are illustrated in Christie's New York sale catalog of October 15, 1985.

No. 16 shown actual size.

13

No. 19. Cup probably by Thomas Hayward (left). *No. 20. Cup by
"TP"* (center). *No. 21. Cup by "RC"* (right).

19–21
THREE GOURD-SHAPED CUPS

19. Probably Thomas Hayward
Salisbury, England, ca. 1670

Hayward's mark and secondary mark at rim
Contemporary engraved initials "·B·/R·S·" on face of finial
H. inc. cover 6⅛"; H. of body 4¾"; Diam. at rim 4¾"
Wgt. 17 oz. 17 dwt.

1972-43

20. Unidentified mark of "TP"
London, 1664/65

Fully marked atop cover and beneath base
Contemporary engraved arms of Doderidge, County
 Devon
H. inc. cover 8⅛"; H. of body 5⅛"; Diam. at rim 5½"
Wgt. 27 oz. 19 dwt.

John A. Hyman Collection, 1987-874

**21. Unidentified mark of "RC" above a pellet
 in a shield**
**Possibly Lincoln or Bury Saint Edmonds,
 England, ca. 1770–1780**

Mark of "RC" and fleurs-de-lis near rim and twice beneath
 base
Sets of engraved initials and dates beginning 1677 beneath
 base
H. 3⅜"; Diam. at rim 4"
Wgt. 9 oz

John A. Hyman Collection, 1989-137

Bellied cups such as these were extremely popular during the reign of Charles II, first appearing around 1660 and continuing for nearly two decades. They vary from the small and plain to the large and luxurious and are usually covered and playfully decorated. The deeply chased designs range from the highly symbolic lion and unicorn, the royal supporters, to hounds, harts, turkeys, thick-leaved flowers, and even an elephant on one Irish example. At least two examples are heavily ornamented with raised classical busts; another is decorated with a realistic hunting scene.

The finial with its four clown masks is specific to this period, as is the flat finial that permits the cover to double as a stand and provides a highly visible place for an engraved armorial. The handles are a development of the earlier, more complex caryatid type (see nos. 1–3).

The origin of small, uncovered, plain versions of this shape seems localized in East Anglia and New England. In New England, this form persisted well into the eighteenth century, serving to remind New Englanders, many of whom emigrated from East Anglia, of their origins. American examples survive in some numbers because they were donated to churches, where they were treated carefully as sacramental vessels.

Davis, *English Silver at Williamsburg*, credits the Hayward cup to John How of Salisbury (p. 58). The present attribution is based on recent research by Timothy Kent, an expert on West Country silver. The "TP" example was advertised by S. J. Shrubsole, London, in *Apollo: The Magazine of the Arts* (CXXV [Feb. 1987], p. 31). The plain-bodied example is illustrated in Christie's New York sale catalog of April 18, 1989.

Detail of no. 21. Though the earliest date and engraved initials are probably contemporary with the cup, the remainder were added later at different times, tracing the cup's descent through a single family over two and one-half centuries.

Detail of no. 19.

22
BRAMPTON MOOR RACING CUP

Unidentified mark of a rose
Possibly Carlisle, England, 1666

Rose mark four times at rim
Contemporary engraved inscription "Brampton Moore
    Course the 25th of March 1666/Sr Richard Sanford"
H. 3"; Diam. at rim 3⅜"
Wgt. 4 oz. 14 dwt.

Formerly in the collections of Sir Walter Gilbey, Bart., and
    Mrs. Oliver Colthurst, John A. Hyman Collection, 1992-
    171

No. 22. Brampton Moor Racing Cup.

This rather ordinary-looking vessel has been called the earliest known English silver racing cup, even though it is a utilitarian vessel in a routine shape and size rather than one designed as a trophy. Michael Clayton notes, "Of these early prizes few are known to have survived. The Brampton Moor Cup of 1666 is perhaps the earliest" (*Collector's Dictionary*, p. 295). Cyril Bunt confirms this claim, dating the next-oldest example, the Asby Maske Cup (a similar shape, with a later cover) three years later (*Apollo: The Magazine of the Arts*, LXXII [1960], p. 142).

Brampton Moor was the site of a typical small country meet, the sort patronized almost entirely by local people to whom the venue was readily accessible. The races were run on public lands, not on the dedicated courses that sprang up all across Britain in the eighteenth century, and certainly not on the enclosed tracks of the nineteenth century. These were modest events, rather like a county fair, with equally modest rewards. A small, locally made silver cup could become a valued prize simply by adding an appropriately engraved inscription. That this was a long-standing practice is seen in the plain baluster mug, another piece of domestic, utilitarian plate, given as a prize at Moulsey Hurst in 1780 (no. 102).

The earliest race meetings, around 1600, fell into three categories: at the court, in the towns, and among the local gentry. Court racing was closed to all but royalty and royalty's hangers-on. Races in the second category, held at towns such as Doncaster and Chester, were financed partly by local corporations and guilds and partly by subscriptions from the local gentry, whose horses were the contenders.

Brampton Moor fell into the third tier, sponsored entirely by the local gentry. Though horse racing was ostensibly the purpose of the meet, the opportunity for serious wagering was the major attraction, whether the race was held at tony Newmarket or on Brampton Moor. Gambling on horse races, cockfights, bowls, cards, or other contests was the primary form of competition among the gentry. The sport made no difference; it was merely an excuse for betting, and heavy losses (though seldom ruinous) were the rule. Reputations and estates could hang in the balance.

It is possible this cup was made by a Carlisle smith, in keeping with the scope of the event. Brampton Moor was an easy ride from Carlisle, the one large town in the area. Sir Richard Sanford, second baronet of Howgill Castle, lived only a few miles away. The rose was an accepted mark for the town, having been used on the coins made when the Carlisle Mint opened in 1654 (certification from Brand Inglis, Oct. 14, 1992).

Illustrated in Walter Gilbey, *Racing Cups, 1559 to 1850: Coursing Cups* ([London, 1910], p. 18).

23
EARLY WINE TASTER

Unidentified mark of "IW" with three pellets between over a billet
London, 1671/72

Fully marked at rim
Contemporary engraved inscription "William Hawkins 1671"
H. ⅞"; Diam. at rim 4"
Wgt. 2 oz. 17 dwt.

John A. Hyman Collection, 1989-52

During the seventeenth century, wine tasters were strictly professional equipment intended for use by wine merchants. They were made of silver because no other material available (pewter, wood,

glass) could withstand the rigors of travel or be depended on to present the wine without contamination. Even two centuries earlier, when the export of silver was forbidden, silver wine tasters used professionally were specifically exempt from the ban: "Provided always that this Act extend not . . . to any Merchant going over the sea to buy any wine to be brought into this Realm, as for (to carry) cariying with him only a little (cup) pece called a Taster (or shewer) for wine" (17 Edward IV c. 1). The few known seventeenth-century wine tasters are uniformly straightforward and sturdy, seldom decorated, lacking handles (to fit in and remove from a pocket without snagging), and domed. The dome is a taster's distinguishing functional element: the merchant evaluates the color and texture of a wine by swirling it over the dome, where it catches the light. Hence the word "shewer" as a synonym for "taster."

Illustrated in Sotheby's London sale catalog of November 17, 1988. Identification and wording of the statute, written in Anglo-Norman French, was furnished by David Beasley, librarian at Goldsmiths' Hall, London.

No. 23. Wine taster.

Clockwise from bottom left: *No. 24. Unmarked miniature.*
No. 25. Miniature by "NI" or "IN." No. 26. Miniature by
"HH." No. 27. Miniature with illegible mark. No. 28.
Miniature by "RS." No. 29. Miniature by "SL."

24–29

SIX EARLY MINIATURES

24. Unmarked
Probably London, ca. 1660

Portrait bust of Charles II and "CR 2" in base
Contemporary scratch-engraved initials "D/T/I" at rim
H. ⅝"; Diam. at rim 2¼"
Wgt. 11 dwt.

John A. Hyman Collection, 1988-175

25. Unidentified mark of "NI" or "IN" with a pellet between
London, 1693/94

Fully marked within bowl
Contemporary engraved initials "EC" on bottom
H. ¾"; Diam. at rim 2³⁄₁₆"
Wgt. 14 dwt.

John A. Hyman Collection, 1988-178

26. Unidentified mark of "HH"
London, 1687/88

Fully marked at rim
H. ¾"; Diam. at rim 2¼"
Wgt. 13 dwt.

John A. Hyman Collection, 1988-182

27. Mark illegible
London, 1707/08

Fully marked on bottom
Britannia standard
H. 1¼"; Diam. at rim 1⅝"
Wgt. 8 dwt.

1970-67

28. Unidentified mark of "RS" above a mullet
London, 1685/86

Fully marked at rim
Contemporary engraved initials "E.T." on bottom
H. 1⁵⁄₁₆"; Diam. at rim 2¹⁄₁₆"
Wgt. 19 dwt.

John A. Hyman Collection, 1988-195

29. Unidentified mark, possibly "SL" in monogram
Probably London, ca. 1665

Fully marked at rim
H. ⅝"; Diam. at rim 2"
Wgt. 12 dwt.

John A. Hyman Collection, 1988-181

These miniatures encompass the history of late seventeenth-century style, a period when they were extraordinarily popular. Sir Charles Jackson describes them as wine tasters (*History of English Plate*, I, p. 216) and the term has stuck, though it is totally inappropriate. Based on the number surviving, if these were wine tasters, every adult in Britain had a palate for wine without parallel, even when compared to our bibulous age.

Some people decry such pieces as flimsy, casually made, and suggestive of inferior workmanship and a lowering of standards. Of greater significance is their broad distribution, as demonstrated by the large number that survive. Most striking is the fact that people had the money to buy these small silver objects, that they were free to make consumer-driven choices, and that there were goods that enabled them to make this sort of fashion statement.

This was popular, stylish silver specifically for the wealthier middle class. Except in Britain and the Netherlands, consumer freedom of this magnitude was unknown in the seventeenth century; elsewhere silver was produced primarily as the result of court or ecclesiastical patronage.

Examples from the 1660s and later are deep chased with stylized flower heads borrowed from Dutch decoration. The European influence is to be expected, inasmuch as styles are often traced to royal preference. In this instance the inclinations of the new king, Charles II, whose tastes had been formed during his Continental exile, prevailed.

Such unsubtle decoration is common to most miniatures, even after it is replaced by more elegant matted bands. These standardized forms of ornamentation reflect not just changing tastes but also a way to economize on labor so goods could be priced to appeal to the broadest possible market. This response to a sort of nouveau riche enthusiasm may explain why much decoration of such miniatures is technically mediocre and unvarying, though with different levels of success.

Both the "SL" and "HH" pieces are illustrated in Sotheby's London sale catalog of October 17, 1985.

Detail of no. 29.

Detail of no. 24. This silver miniature is an amazing rarity. It was made to fit a stamped medallion bearing the likeness of King Charles II, issued to commemorate his return to the English throne in 1660. To fit the medallion, the round bowl has an oval bottom. Its condition is splendid, showing how its owners must have treasured it across many generations. Stuart loyalties run deep.

30

BOWL IN IBERIAN STYLE

Unidentified mark of "N L" with a pellet
   between
London, 1689/90

Fully marked at rim plus; unidentifiable fifth mark at rim
With contemporary engraved initials "* E */I* S" at rim
H. 1¼"; Diam. at rim 3¼"; L. over handles 4⅜"
Wgt. 1 oz. 11 dwt.

Formerly in the collection of Mrs. Robert W. Gouinlock,
   Toronto, Canada, John A. Hyman Collection, 1993-60

No. 30. Bowl by "N L."

In its workmanship and design of prominent chased lobes and coarse punched decoration, this bowl resembles examples from half a century earlier (see nos. 4 and 5), but its design may stem from a different impulse. The earlier examples are decorated superficially with no attempt to show depth, whereas this design appears to simulate the highly dimensional lobes used to decorate English bowls in the middle of the century, a type of decoration probably adapted from Portuguese forms. In fact, because of its dimensionality, this bowl seems more Iberian than English, just as the handles reflect outside influences in the way they tuck into the bowl rather than roll out in the expected English scroll.

Illustrated in Sotheby's New York sale catalog of April 23, 1993. A similarly handled example, with similar scale-type chasing but without the punched decoration, is illustrated in Jackson, *History of English Plate* (II, p. 739). The Burrell Collection (Glasgow, Scotland) has two splendid mid-seventeenth century English bowls with bodies similar to this one, except the decoration was worked by shaping the metal rather than merely chasing it. The Burrell Collection bowls are also considerably larg-

er than this one. Perhaps physically shaping the metal was reserved for more important objects, with chasing used to achieve the same effect with less effort on lesser pieces. Another large example, dated 1656/57, also has a shaped (rather than chased) bowl and is illustrated in Hackenbroch, *Silver in the Untermyer Collection* (pl. 42).

31
SEVENTEENTH-CENTURY TUMBLER

William Mathew
London, 1671/72

Fully marked beneath body
Contemporary engraved arms of Thornagh of Fenton,
 County Nottinghamshire, quartering Ferres and others,
 possibly Zouch and Skeffington; later scratched invento-
 ry mark "14/P" beneath body
H. 3"; Diam. at rim 4"
Wgt. 9 oz. 13 dwt.

John A. Hyman Collection, 1992-128

The extraordinary character of this magnificent tumbler cannot be conveyed by an illustration; it must be encountered, seen, and held. It invests this simplest of all forms with an inexplicable magnetism. Hold it, and it commands all of your attention. It fills your hand. It is both dynastic and Dionysian.

There may not be another seventeenth-century example of such majesty. A smaller example that is nonetheless considerable in size and quality is shown in Wark, *British Silver in the Huntington Collection* (p. 18), but its engraved arms lack the certainty and spreading strength of this incisive armorial. A 1708 tumbler in the Untermyer Collection stands almost an inch taller and weighs an amazing thirteen ounces, seven pennyweight, but, because it is vertical in the eighteenth-century manner, it lacks the virility of this example (Hackenbroch, *Silver in the Untermyer Collection*, fig. 104). A pair of Irish tumblers with a total weight of more than twenty-two ounces was sold by Sotheby's of London on April 20, 1972. Made by Robert Goble in Cork around 1680, they are primitive, squat, and strongly shaped, but Goble's attempt at a conven-

tional cartouche resulted in a childlike fountain instead of tied plumes.

Illustrated in Sotheby's London sale catalog of November 1, 1990. This cup's exceptional size and weight and superb proportions can best be appreciated by comparing it to the group of ten tumblers, spanning the history of the form, Wark, *British Silver in the Huntington Collection* (pp. 18–21).

No. 31. Tumbler by William Mathew.

No. 32. Nest of tumblers by "RH."

32
NEST OF TUMBLERS

Unidentified mark of "RH" with a pellet
  between
London, ca. 1680

"RH" on bottom of each tumbler (twice on largest)
Silver gilt
H. inc. cover 3"; H. of tumblers 2³⁄₁₆"–2½"; Diam. of cover
  3⁵⁄₁₆"; Diam. of tumblers 2¾"–3³⁄₁₆"
Total wgt. 12 oz. 18 dwt.

Formerly in the collections of the earl of Home, H. H.
  Mulliner, and William Randolph Hearst, 1938-22, 1-7

This amazing set probably served as part of a
travel canteen carried within a shagreen or leather
case. The wonderful soft gilding is unconventional.
The matted bands are a typical decorative element,
but they are rarely seen divided so carefully into
panels. The gilding, the quality of the matting, and
the attention to detail shown in the paneled decoration all indicate a client important enough to be
served with more than ordinary plate and with
specialized objects for travel.

The only other known set of nesting tumblers
is in the Untermyer Collection at the Metropolitan
Museum of Art in New York City. This set also has
a lid as well as its original case. With few exceptions, surviving tumblers are lidless, and we cannot
tell how many were regularly supplied with lids.
With time, the lids were probably separated from
the bodies and lost, discarded, or melted down so
that the metal could be reused, especially if the feet
had broken off of the lid.

Illustrated with additional references in Davis,
English Silver at Williamsburg (pp. 51–53). The
Untermyer nest is illustrated in Hackenbroch, *Silver
in the Untermyer Collection* (pl. 74).

Nest shown closed.

33–36
FOUR TUMBLERS

33. Unmarked
Presumably England, probably 1748

Applewood, silver band at rim
Contemporary engraved inscriptions "ROYAL OAK" and
   "Sr Richd Acton of Aldenham Bart 1748" on band
H. 2¼"; Diam. at rim 3⅛"

John A. Hyman Collection, 1990-201

34. John Payne
London, 1751/52

Fully marked at rim
Gilt interior
H. 2⁵⁄₁₆"; Diam. at rim 2¾"
Wgt. 4 oz.

1955-105

35. Maker's mark illegible
London, 1718/19

Fully marked on bottom
Contemporary engraved initials "I*P" at rim; elaborate
   contemporary engraved cipher
H. 2⅛"; Diam. at rim 2⁹⁄₁₆"
Wgt. 3 oz. 13 dwt.

1990-135

36. William Fleming
London, 1714/15

Fully marked at rim
Britannia standard, gilt interior
Contemporary engraved cipher
H. 1¾"; Diam. at rim 2¾"
Wgt. 2 oz. 6 dwt.

John A. Hyman Collection, 1991-600

The tumbler is the simplest of all silver vessels: a plain bowl with a rounded bottom weighted with an extra thickness of silver. It is associated

Clockwise from left: *No. 33. Unmarked tumbler. No. 34. Tumbler by John Payne. No. 35. Tumbler with illegible mark. No. 36. Tumbler by William Fleming.*

with strong waters and companionable imbibing. Put down your tumbler after tossing down a draft and it rights itself, even when placed at the same precarious angle as the drinker.

Tumblers as small as the Fleming example are quite rare. The form remains consistent over time, modestly altered in size or proportion to follow changes in style, but never as drastically as larger vessels such as mugs or tankards. The earliest known tumblers date from the mid-seventeenth century and have a resolute shape, wider than tall. Eighteenth-century examples are more vertical. The few tumblers that strive to keep up with fashion do so by adding the decoration of the moment. When the ornamentation challenges the purity of the form, for example, when chased gadroons are added, the results are seldom satisfactory.

Perhaps because it is such a simple form, the tumbler provides a wonderful vehicle for the engraver's handiwork: elaborate armorials or ciphers in formal surrounds are cleanly presented. The example with the delicate floral engraving is exceptional, probably because the tumbler form is so masculine and is often seen with inscriptions such as "The Foreman's Oath," "Success to the Mines," or to memorialize competitions.

Sir Richard Acton, the original owner of the treen tumbler, was unusually inactive for a country squire. He never ran for Parliament and never served in the navy. He held only one local office, sheriff of Salop, and that only briefly from 1751 to 1752 (telephone conversation with heraldic specialist Gale Glynn, Nov. 4, 1990). The engraved inscription "ROYAL OAK" suggests Sir Richard was a Jacobite (Stuart monarchist) sympathizer because it is dated only two years after the disaster at Culloden, where the British routed the Scots under the Young Pretender, Bonnie Prince Charlie. "Royal Oak" probably refers to the Boscobel Oak, an icon of Jacobite sentiment.

The Payne tumbler is illustrated in Davis, *English Silver at Williamsburg* (p. 53).

37
EARLY U-BODY CUP

Unidentified mark of "DR" above a pellet
  and below a coronet
London, 1668/69

Fully marked at rim
Contemporary engraved arms of Ettrick of Holt Lodge, in
  the Forest, County Dorset, and later of High Barns,
  County Durham; contemporary engraved letters "R" and
  "G" flanking the arms; contemporary engraved inscrip-
  tion "Ex dono Luciae Ettrick/1665" beneath the arms;
  contemporary scratch-engraved initials "*P*/*IE *"
  beneath the body
H. 3½"; Diam. at rim 4½"
Wgt. 8 oz. 10 dwt.

John A. Hyman Collection, 1992-22

No. 37. Cup by "DR."

This cup is one of a rare few from the early
development of the English U-shaped body made
without a foot. It has survived in good condition
because it was made with a slightly domed bottom
so it could rest on its outer shoulder. Dressed only
in a bravura armorial and set off by exquisitely
complex handles with fish scale decoration and
wonderful dolphin heads, it is gratifying for its
purity.

The simple U-shaped body is a particularly
English silver form that served as a tailored counterpoint to the immensely popular, flamboyant
Dutch baroque designs based on the gourd shape
(see nos. 19–22). Common to English decorative
vessels for half a century, this form served as the
unobtrusive vehicle for a series of stylistic developments. It was decorated with cut-card overlays (see
no. 43), with chased acanthus and palm leaves (see
nos. 38 and 39), with chinoiseries (see nos. 40 and
41), and with swirling gadroons and a roped girdle
(see no. 48).

One element seems constant during the development of the U-bodied cup: smaller examples
were made without covers, large ones with them.
The conservatively made form also retained the
same basic shape for at least three decades. These
cups were probably intended for use and show by
the gentry and successful members of the merchant
class, who often lived outside of London, where
they did not need to change with every fleeting
fashion.

A fine covered example, similarly footless,
dated 1668/69 is illustrated in Wark, *British Silver
in the Huntington Collection* (p. 11), and in Oman,
Caroline Silver (pl. 14B).

*No. 38. Cup by "IN" (left). No. 39. Cup probably by Thomas
Hayward (right).*

38–39

TWO ACANTHUS-CHASED CUPS

38. Unidentified mark of "IN" above a device and within a heart
London, 1678/79

Fully marked atop cover and on body at rim
Silver gilt
Contemporary engraved arms of Lucy of Charlecot, Warwickshire, on body; slightly later engraved initials "*/*E*B*/*" beneath base
H. inc. cover 7⅛"; H. of body 4⅝"; Diam. at rim 6⅜"
Wgt. 32 oz. 12 dwt.

Formerly in the collections of Lord Braye, H. H. Mulliner, and William Randolph Hearst, 1938-30

39. Probably Thomas Hayward
Salisbury, England, 1670–1685

Hayward's mark in monogram and two punches of fleur-de-lis on bottom
Traces of gilt interior
Contemporary engraved armorial of Clark(e) on body; scratch-engraved initials and date on bottom: "*W*/*I*G*/C M/1684"
H. 2⅞"; Diam. at rim 3½"
Wgt. 3 oz. 15 dwt.

Formerly in the collection of the Hudson's Bay Company, John A. Hyman Collection, 1988-196

The squared-off U-shaped body appeared around 1660 (see no. 37) and continued into the following century. Many early examples are chased with a pattern of alternating acanthus and palm leaves, a convention used on vessels of every description, including beakers, tankards, and tumblers. The body was the basis for many variations. One replaced the finial with three scrolled feet so that the cover could be inverted for use as a stand. Another replaced chased decoration with flat silver overlays cut into decorative patterns known as cut-card work (see no. 43).

In its strength and elegance, the massive larger cup yields to few others. Only the most profound examples, such as the Dolben Cup of 1678/79, which stands eleven and one-half inches high and weighs a staggering 134½ ounces, challenges it. (The Dolben Cup is illustrated in Commander How's *Notes* [Summer 1943], p. 4.)

The larger cup is illustrated with additional references in Davis, *English Silver at Williamsburg* (pp. 60–61). The smaller cup is illustrated in Sotheby's New York sale catalog of December 12, 1985.

No. 40. Cup by "RC" (left). No. 41. Cup probably by John Sutton (right).

40–41

TWO CHINOISERIE CUPS

40. Unidentified mark of "RC"
London, ca. 1685

"RC" twice on bezel of cover and thrice on body
Contemporary engraved arms of Hales Family of Wood-
    church, County Kent, and Hales's Place, Canterbury;
    engraved initials "R*G/*/M*N" beneath base
H. inc. cover 6⅞"; H. of body 4½"; Diam. at rim 5½"
Wgt. 22 oz. 7 dwt.

John A. Hyman Collection, 1987-875

41. Probably John Sutton
London, 1692/93

Fully marked on bottom
Contemporary scratch-engraved initials "P/I M" on bottom
H. 2½"; Diam. at rim 3¹⁄₁₆"
Wgt. 3 oz. 17 dwt.

John A. Hyman Collection, 1988-197

The difference between these cups and numbers 37–39 is not as radical as it seems. All are based on the U-shaped body, and the larger acanthus-chased cup (no. 38) has a similar cover. Here, the larger "RC" cup (no. 40) sports a very English cartouche to provide space for identifying armorials—the English who could afford major pieces of silver saw each piece as a vehicle for personal aggrandizement, regardless of stylistic compatibility. The twig-and-bark handles illustrate the way a stylized element like the caryatid handle (see nos. 1, 2, 3, and 19–21) could transform itself in response to changing fashion.

These cups illustrate the radical shift into fanciful, lighthearted, two-dimensional imaginary vistas known as "chinoiseries." English interest in oriental decorative arts began during the reign of

Elizabeth I with porcelains and lacquers, the growth of the silk trade, and the importation of tea. What could be more fashionable than drinking tea (and more potent liquors—see no. 84) in a Chinese context?

How do we interpret such exotic depictions of a world that never was, populated with strange birds, odd people in theatrical poses, dragons, and fountains set amid extraordinary flora? Certainly, stolid English realists saw such renderings as fancies, follies, entertainments, and caricatures. Were these images a metaphor for the superiority of English customs and attitudes, in contrast to the hedonism of a heathen people in a picturesque, purportedly carefree, utterly different land?

Chinoiserie designs appeared in cycles. They were popular for less than two decades at the end of the seventeenth century, when they were splashed everywhere: on cups and mugs of all types and sizes, toilet articles, large bowls, and salvers. They returned to favor fifty years later, thematically related to the baroque examples shown here but in rococo dress and thus different in appearance.

Much has been written about these delightful designs, the most definitive article being Carl Christian Dauterman's "Dream Pictures of Cathay: Chinoiserie on Restoration Silver" (Metropolitan Museum of Art, *Bulletin*, XXIII [Summer 1964], pp. 11–25). Dauterman believes that this briefly popular decoration can be traced to no more than one or two specialist chasers who decorated pieces for a large number of London silversmiths.

The smaller cup is illustrated in Brett, *Sotheby's Directory of Silver* (p. 137), and in Sotheby's New

York sale catalog of December 28, 1968. What may be the finest collection of chinoiseries assembled during the twentieth century is found in the beautifully illustrated sale catalog (with an introductory essay by Philippa Glanville of the Victoria and Albert Museum) of the Jaime Ortiz-Patino collection, Sotheby's New York, May 21, 1992. Each example is remarkable for the vigor and complexity of its exquisitely detailed and crisp decoration. The collection includes tankards, monteiths, candlesticks, scent flasks, covered bowls and cups, mugs, snuffers and stands, a looking glass, and a toilet service.

Reverse of no. 40.

EARLY SCOTTISH COVERED CUP

No. 42. Cup by James Penman.

James Penman
Edinburgh, 1693/94

Fully marked beneath cover and beneath bottom, assay
    master John Borthwick
Contemporary engraved mirror cipher "JMC"; later
    engraved arms of Campbell of Netherplace, County Ayr
H. inc. cover 7½"; H. of body 5¼"; Diam. of body 5¾"
Wgt. 28 oz. 14 dwt.

John A. Hyman Collection, 1992-130

This elegant cup is probably the earliest of a
small group of large, splendid covered cups made
in Edinburgh from around 1690 to 1715. Each has a
stepped lid, a U-shaped body, and a small applied
knob atop each handle. The latter feature seems
unique to this group. This is the only example with
strap, rather than hollow, handles and a wrought
foot and is the only one that is relatively free of
English influence.

This cup, vested with the beauty of simplicity,
is the one member of the group that reads horizon-
tally. The cover is flatter, the foot less prominent,
and the slim handles swing wide in a generous
curve to meet the body at an unusually low point.
In an unconsciously graceful way, they form a lovely
heart.

The handles form a perfect counterpoint to the
body, the foot provides an unobtrusive anchor, and
the cover augments the piece's breadth in a studied
geometry to which nothing can be added and from
which little can be subtracted. Originating as it did
during a period when superficial ornament out-
weighed geometry, when handles, feet, and covers
were often clichés added without thought of cohe-
sion, it is amazing to find a vessel whose simple

severity and superb balance imbue it with the utmost dignity.

This covered cup was illustrated in Sotheby's catalog for the Hopetoun House sale of November 13, 1978. It also appears in the revised edition of Finlay, *Scottish Gold and Silver Work*, together with two slightly later cups (one with a spout) from this group that show how Huguenot concepts (see no. 43) affected Scottish forms as early as the first decade of the century (pls. 60, 65, and 66). For another example of Huguenot influence, see William Ged's baluster mug (no. 97).

Detail of no. 42. The engraved motto below the armorial conforms to English style rather than the general Scottish practice of placing the motto at the top.

43

PAIR OF CUT-CARD CUPS

Thomas Bolton
Dublin, 1694/95

Bolton's mark, Hibernia, and date letter on bezel of each
    cover; Bolton's mark, Hibernia, and harp crowned
    beneath each body
Contemporary engraved arms of an unmarried lady of the
    Alanson family on each body; scratched weight
    "11=3=12" beneath one body, "11=-1=12" beneath the
    other
H. inc. cover 4¾"; H. of body 3⅛"; Diam. at rim 3¼"
Total wgt. 21 oz. 18 dwt.

John A. Hyman Collection, 1991-605, 1 & 2

No. 43. Cups by Thomas Bolton.

Cut-card overlays adorn some of the most agreeable examples of English silver. First seen in limited use earlier in the seventeenth century, this form of decoration gained popularity around 1680 because of its appropriateness for the new Huguenot-influenced style (more vertical body; clearly defined foot; cast handles, foot, and midband; and a domed cover). It continued in favor for a brief period until it was replaced by more elaborate, multidimensional, discontinuous cast ornament (see nos. 116 and 117). The creation of cut-card decoration is simple: a flat piece of silver, sometimes shaped to conform to the object it will embellish, is cut to a pattern, then applied over a plain surface in a continuous band, adding dimension as well as decoration. Cut-card overlays in patterns that follow naturalistic shapes in an agreeably tailored manner are especially attractive on cup covers and bodies.

Bolton began with the simplest of all shapes, a plain hemisphere. He graced it with exquisite proportions, a small stepped foot, an elegant cast handle, and a single row of gadroons on the cover. By the judicious addition of a restrained cut-card calyx on the bowl and cover, he imbued his design with dignity and elegance.

Bolton was the most brilliant smith to emerge during the flowering of Irish silverwork that began in the late seventeenth century. He was amazingly versatile, at home with all styles from the baroque to the ultimate in Huguenot sophistication. He was comfortable with a seemingly limitless number of forms: toilet articles, cups, jugs, tea canisters, stands. For one of his large covered cups, decorated in a vastly different style that required a more extensive ornamental vocabulary and the technique to carry it off, see number 49.

A broad assortment of Bolton's work is illustrated in Davis, *Genius of Irish Silver* (pp. 20–22, 34–39).

44–47
SPOUT CUPS AND RELATED MUG

44. William Andrews
London, 1697/98

Fully marked on bottom
Britannia standard
H. 2⅝"; Diam. at rim 3"
Wgt. 5 oz. 1 dwt.

John A. Hyman Collection, 1989-364

45. John East
London, 1713/14

East's mark on cover; fully marked on body
Britannia standard
Contemporary engraved initials "*M*/R*S" on body
H. inc. cover 4½"; H. of body 2⅞"; Diam. at rim 3⅜"
Wgt. 6 oz. 8 dwt.

John A. Hyman Collection, 1988-199

46. Unidentified mark of crowned "G" above
three mullets
Probably London, before 1690

Mark of "G" thrice on bottom
Contemporary engraved arms of Elizabeth, widow of Sir
    James Phelps of Barrington, County Somerset, extinct in
    1690
H. 2⅝"; Diam. at rim 3¼"
Wgt. 5 oz. 12 dwt.

Formerly in the collection of the Hudson's Bay Company,
    John A. Hyman Collection, 1988-198

47. William Fleming
London, 1722/23

Fleming's mark on underside of handle; fully marked on
    bottom
Britannia standard
Contemporary initials (partly scratched out) and date
    "1723" on bottom
H. 1⅞"; Diam. at rim 2³⁄₁₆"
Wgt. 1 oz. 14 dwt.

John A. Hyman Collection, 1990-61

Clockwise from left: *No. 44. Cup by William Andrews. No. 45.*
Cup by John East. No. 46. Cup by "G." No. 47. Mug by William
Fleming.

According to Michael Clayton, the earliest English personal drinking vessels were spout cups; he mentions one dated 1640 and another from 1642 (*Collector's Dictionary*, p. 385). Because they were made with handles at right angles to the spout (easier for drinking than pouring), such small cups may have been vessels for feeding invalids. They were more probably used for posset, a drink consisting of curdled milk, spices, and beer or wine. The milk rose to the top while the palatable part remained at the bottom and poured through the conveniently located spout. The spout cup is a derivative form adapted from conventional drinking shapes such as tankards, beakers, or bellied mugs (whichever was in fashion at the time), as is easily seen by comparing the Andrews spout cup with the Fleming mug. There was little visual consistency except in New England, where a standard form evolved based on a bellied mug with a reeded neck augmented by a spout, cover, and sometimes a beaded handle.

The broad, flat handles on the Andrews spout cup and the Fleming mug were easily made, highly practical, and comforting in the way they hugged the user's fingers when he or she needed to steady the vessel. This type of handle can be seen at least a quarter-century earlier on a similarly plain exampled dated 1673/74.

The Andrews spout cup is illustrated in Christie's London sale catalog of October 25, 1989. The "crowned G" example is illustrated in Sotheby's New York sale catalog of December 12, 1985. Another John East spout cup, virtually identical in size and shape and dated 1717/18, is illustrated in Davis, *English Silver at Williamsburg* (p. 198). Michael

Clayton shows many of the rarest and most interesting spout cups in *Collector's Dictionary* (p. 385). The silver mug of 1673/74 was illustrated by Donohoe, the London dealer, in *Country Life* (CLXXXVI [Sept. 10, 1992], p. 57).

Detail of no. 44.

Detail of no. 46.

BAROQUE COVERED CUP

Robert Timbrell
London, 1693/94

Timbrell's mark four times beneath cover; fully marked
  beneath base
Contemporary engraved initials "L/*I*I*" beneath base
H. inc. cover 6⅜"; H. of body 4⅜"; Diam. at rim 5⅛"
Wgt. 16 oz. 11 dwt.

John A. Hyman Collection, 1987-832

This compact cup epitomizes the versatility of the U-shaped body (see nos. 37–41) and its accommodation of a wide variety of decorative schemes. The earlier calyx of acanthus and palm leaves has been replaced by swirling flutes and gadroons under a ropelike girdle. As on the earlier cups, the decoration appears on both the body and the cover.

The first visual difference between this cup and earlier examples is geometric: the chasing is in constant movement, unlike the static, vertical designs that preceded it. The second difference is more subtle: the deeply chased lobes are offset by shallow, punched foliate patterns that soften the contrast between the smooth body and the highly dimensional ornament. This is an early step toward the alternation of textures that the Huguenots exploited to great effect beginning around 1690 and continued for nearly four decades, though with radically different styling made possible by updated technology (see nos. 116 and 117).

Advertised by S. J. Shrubsole, New York, in *The Magazine Antiques* (CXXX [1986], p. 361).

No. 48. Cup by Robert Timbrell.

49

THOMAS BOLTON COVERED CUP

Thomas Bolton
Dublin, 1699/1700

Harp crowned and date letter beneath cover; fully marked
  beneath base
Unidentified contemporary engraved arms on body;
  engraved weight "60=7=12" beneath base
H. inc. cover 10⅝"; H. of body 7⅜"; Diam. at rim 7³⁄₁₆"
Wgt. 58 oz.

John A. Hyman Collection, 1987-876

This stately cup heralds both a new century
and the transition from the U-shaped bowl to the
inverted bell shape that replaced it. The cover is
now a double-stepped dome, the body is belted
close to the waist, the foot has become a separate
element, and the handles assume greater dimensionality and are heavily ornamented. Although
Bolton was an early exponent of the new styles and
had already mastered the sensibility required for
them (beautifully illustrated by the pair of cups
made five years earlier—see no. 43), he continued
to employ elements representative of the last major
type of chased decoration in the Anglo-Dutch tradition. Here, at a time when Anglo-French overlaid
ornament had begun to affect silver design, the use
of broad bands of continuous fluting in the Anglo-
Dutch style of worked sheet metal is almost anachronistic.

Bolton's work is uniformly splendid, albeit
sometimes quirkily individualistic. For example,
the loosely flowing band at the girdle, suggestive of
windblown wheat sheaves, appears on other Bolton
cups; one of 1700 was illustrated in a Garrard & Co.
advertisement in *Apollo* (LXIII [Jan. 1956], p. i). This
detail is entirely at odds with the rigid up-and-
down patterns favored by most Irish and English
smiths and employed by Bolton on other examples.

No. 49. Cup by Thomas Bolton.

This cup is illustrated in Sassoon, *Loan Exhibition of Old English Plate* (pl. XLV), in Christie's London sale catalog of June 15, 1983, and in S. J. Shrubsole's (New York) advertisement in *The Magazine Antiques* (CXXXI [1987], p. 505). It was previously sold at Christie's London on June 21, 1922. An engagingly small Bolton covered cup with a more disciplined (and more typical) girdle is illustrated in Wark, *British Silver in the Huntington Collection* (p. 13).

Detail of no. 49.

50–51
TWO LOFTHOUSE FAMILY CUPS

50. Matthew Lofthouse
London, 1711/12

Fully marked on bezel of cover and at rim
Britannia standard
Contemporary unidentified engraved armorial within
   cartouche
H. inc. cover 9¼"; H. of body 6"; Diam. at rim 6"
Wgt. 31 oz. 15 dwt.

Formerly in the collection of Eric N. Shrubsole, John A.
   Hyman Collection, 1992-162

There are few finer examples of the English baroque—florid, energized, and dramatic—at its pinnacle. This glorious cup by a member of the prolific Lofthouse family of silversmiths includes every element of the style: a profusion of swirling gadroons and flutes (on the foot, body, cover, and finial); a prominent, corded midband that intersects an oversized, boldly conceived cartouche textured with fish scales and matting; horizontals emphasized by parallel lines of irregularly placed, stamped foliate decoration; an emphasis on dimension and the play of light and shadow; and variation between textures. None of the standard techniques for achieving the characteristics of the ornate English baroque style is lacking here.

Matthew Lofthouse was trapped in a stylistic gap when he created this cup. The old, squarish Anglo-Dutch style with its heavily chased decoration and wrought handles was on the wane but had not been replaced fully by the Continental style recently introduced by the Huguenots (see no. 114). Trying to synthesize the two, Lofthouse created a series of compromises between the proportion and decoration he knew best and what was probably

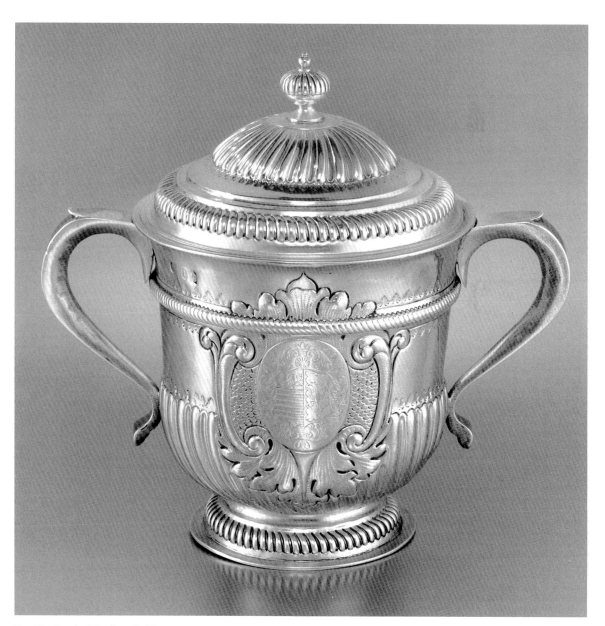

No. 50. Cup by Matthew Lofthouse.

demanded by his clients. The decoration is a perfect statement of his finest work, but the plain handles (an attempt to simulate the new cast style) fail to frame the body with appropriate strength. The cover and foot look to both the old style and the new and as a result lack the resolution needed to balance the composition.

This cup can help us understand how difficult it was for native English smiths, confined by their insular style and limited technology, to adjust to suddenly changed aesthetics. Nevertheless, if Lofthouse failed in his compromise, he still delivered a brilliantly worked drinking vessel that has enormous presence, which was his stylistic and social purpose.

As a transitional form, this cup is best understood when compared to what came before, the Timbrell covered cup of 1693/94 (no. 48), and after, the Buteux covered cup of 1727/28 (no. 115). Buteux, whose output epitomizes the Huguenot tradition, could also work in the Anglo-Dutch fashion when a client called on him to do so. Thus, Sir Charles Jackson refers to an Abraham Buteux porringer (a large covered cup) of 1724/25 as "spiral flutings and repousse shield" (*English Goldsmiths and Their Marks*, p. 178). In his turn, Lofthouse made baluster mugs that could be easily mistaken for work by a Huguenot smith. Regardless of their training and instinct, smiths had to accommodate each client's stylistic demands; they were never totally in one camp during this transitional period.

51. Mary Lofthouse
London, 1730/31

Fully marked on bottom
Contemporary engraved initials "I/T:M" within cartouche
H. 3¾"; Diam. at rim 4½"
Wgt. 7 oz. 17 dwt.

John A. Hyman Collection, 1987-878

Made two decades later, Mary Lofthouse's cup is a literal replication of Matthew Lofthouse's magnificent covered cup, far smaller in size but with every detail except the cover in place. It may be less crisply executed, perhaps because it was less ambitious or because smiths had lost their intimacy with the style.

Mary Lofthouse was a widow when she entered her mark at Goldsmiths' Hall on March 30, 1731. A widow could succeed her husband and continue his shop, using her own mark in the lozenge shape that denoted an unmarried lady (a priv-

No. 51. Cup by Mary Lofthouse.

ilege customarily granted to widows of Guild members), though most widows probably served as business rather than working partners. Mary's husband may have been Matthew Lofthouse, who opened his shop in 1687, or Matthew's older brother Seth, who had a separate shop around the same time. Both Matthew and Seth turned out serviceable, mainstream goods (Grimwade, *London Goldsmiths*, pp. 584–585). Although they kept up with the newest fashions, the Lofthouses probably also catered to a small body of customers who clung to familiar styles, probably members of the middle class who were defensive about things that smacked of foreign influence. Otherwise, how can one account for a cup so anachronistic?

Though it is known that Mary entered her mark in 1731, this piece has been dated 1730/31 because date letters did not coincide with the calendar year. Before 1660, the date letter was changed each May 19 in honor of Saint Dunstan, the patron saint of goldsmiths. With the return of the Stuart monarchy (and the prospect of royal patronage) in 1660, the date letter was changed to May 29 to honor the birthday of King Charles II. In highly symbolic fashion, May 29 was also the date the king returned from exile.

This type of cup is sometimes called a "caudle cup" in the belief that it was the vessel of choice for a popular drink of the late seventeenth century. Michael Clayton has described white caudle as a gruel-like mixture of oatmeal, spices, and white wine. Brown caudle substituted ale, red wine, or brandy for the white wine, and tea caudle, which may have been a tonic for pregnant women, had a tea base with eggs added to it (*Collector's Dictionary*, p. 78).

Sotheby's New York sale catalog of October 28, 1983, attributes this cup to Matthew Lofthouse.

Clockwise from left: *No. 52. Miniature by George Beale.*
No. 53. Miniature by Benjamin Bentley. No. 54. Minia-
ture by "NL." No. 55. Miniature by "IN" or "NI." No.
56. Miniature by "HE."

52–56

FIVE LATER MINIATURES

52. George Beale
London, 1705/06

Fully marked on bottom
Britannia standard
H. 1¾"; Diam. at rim 1⅝"
Wgt. 16 dwt.

John A. Hyman Collection, 1988-194

53. Benjamin Bentley
London, 1713/14

Fully marked on bottom
Britannia standard
H. 1½"; Diam. at rim 2"
Wgt. 18 dwt.

John A. Hyman Collection, 1988-187

54. Unidentified mark of "NL"
London, 1693/94

Fully marked at rim
H. 1⁹⁄₁₆"; Diam. at rim 1¹³⁄₁₆"
Wgt. 18 dwt.

John A. Hyman Collection, 1988-190

55. Unidentified mark of "IN" or "NI" with a pellet between
London, 1694/95

Fully marked on bottom
H. 1¼"; Diam. at rim 1⅞"
Wgt. 14 dwt.

Formerly in the collection of Mrs. C. J. Devine, Sr., John A. Hyman Collection, 1988-192

56. Unidentified mark of "HE" conjoined
London, 1690/91

Fully marked at rim
H. ¾"; Diam. at rim 2"
Wgt. 9 dwt.

John A. Hyman Collection, 1988-193

These miniatures take up the history of style where numbers 24–29 leave off, as the seventeenth century draws to a close. The pieces pictured here show how stylistic change was reflected in all objects, whether large and ostentatious or small and unambitious. They also come in greater diversity: cups, mugs, and bowls.

The Beale mug with its round body differs from the others visually and functionally. It represents a new form, the true mug, and is described by Peter Waldron as "the earliest type of mug you are likely to come across" (*Price Guide to Antique Silver*, p. 187). For larger examples of this form, see numbers 84–89.

The "NI/IN" cup is illustrated in Christie's New York sale catalog of October 15, 1985.

57–59

THREE PROVINCIAL MINIATURES

57. Colin McKenzie
Edinburgh, ca. 1695

McKenzie's mark on bottom
H. 1½"; Diam. at rim 1⁹⁄₁₆"
Wgt. 1 oz. 3 dwt.

John A. Hyman Collection, 1990-130

58. Thomas Walker or Thomas Williamson
Dublin, ca. 1730

Walker or Williamson's mark, Hibernia, harp crowned on bottom
H. 1⁷⁄₁₆"; Diam. at rim 2¹⁄₁₆"
Wgt. 1 oz. 8 dwt.

John A. Hyman Collection, 1988-189

59. Joseph Walker
Dublin, ca. 1700

Walker's mark on bottom
Contemporary engraved initials "M*D" on side
H. 1⅜"; Diam. at rim 1⅝"
Wgt. 1 oz.

Formerly in the collection of Dr. Kurt Ticher, John A. Hyman Collection, 1990-129

No. 57. Miniature by Colin McKenzie (left). No. 58. Miniature by Thomas Walker or Thomas Williamson (center). No. 59. Miniature by Joseph Walker.

McKenzie's thistle cup presents this particularly Scottish form at its most decorative. Thistle cups come in a variety of sizes: pint and half-pint down to miniatures such as this. The latter are, according to Commander How's *Notes,* "exceedingly rare" ([Summer 1942], p. 10). This example is fully ornamented with a midband and a calyx of vertical applied tongues. Other examples may be simpler, but nothing can obscure such a graceful and well-proportioned form.

The thistle cup is only one of several forms of drinking vessel that the Scots developed as their own. The quaich (see nos. 60–63) is another form closely linked to Scotland. The true thistle cup, however, is specifically Scottish. Ian Finlay comments that, though it reflects tendencies toward body shapes that are seen elsewhere, "it is surprising that nothing like [the thistle cup] occurs beyond the borders of Scotland" (*Scottish Gold and Silver Work,* p. 120). For a full-sized example, also with an ornamental calyx, see number 89.

The Walker/Williamson Irish cup is lusty to a degree lacking in English examples (see nos. 24–29 and 52–56), with fully detailed cast caryatid handles whose like is seldom seen on miniatures. The more disciplined Joseph Walker cup follows conventional Irish design as seen on large examples of the period. The band of running foliage above the flutes is an especially Irish decorative treatment. A large, circa 1730 example by Mark Fallon of Galway has virtually identical decoration (illustrated in Christie's New York sale catalog of October 15, 1985).

The McKenzie thistle cup is illustrated in Phillips' London sale catalog of April 27, 1990. The Joseph Walker cup is illustrated in Christie's London sale catalog of March 17, 1987, and in Sotheby's New York sale catalog of April 27, 1990. Its previous owner, the late Dr. Kurt Ticher, was a collector, student, and author specializing in Irish silver. His best-known publication is *Irish Silver in the Rococo Period* (Shannon, Ire., 1972).

60–63
FOUR SCOTTISH QUAICHS

60. Unmarked
Probably Scotland, ca. 1750

Laburnum wood, silver mounts and boss
Contemporary engraved motto "God Blesse the/Prince
   Steuart/of Scotland" on boss
H. 1⅞"; Diam. at rim 4"; L. over handles 6"

John A. Hyman Collection, 1991-137

61. Unmarked
Probably Scotland, bowl ca. 1700, mounts and boss ca. 1740

Ebonized beech and fruitwood, silver mounts and boss
Contemporary engraved crest and motto "NUNQUAM
   NON PARATUS" of Johnston and initials "K I" on one
   handle; contemporary engraved crest and motto
   "VINCERE VEL MORI" of McDougall or McDowall and
   initials "AMcD" on the other handle; later (ca. 1780)
   engraved motto "NEC.TEMPORE.NEC.FATO" and
   arms of MacDonald impaling (possibly) Ord on boss

H. 2"; Diam. at rim 4⅝"; L. over handles 6¾"

Formerly in the collection of David Morris, John A. Hyman
   Collection, 1991-174

62. Peter Aitken
Glasgow, ca. 1820

Oak body, maple handles, silver mounts
Contemporary engraved inscriptions: "From Hew Aitken/
   Air" under one handle; "To/D Aird Esqr./Jamaica"
   under the other handle; "The Oak of which this Cup is
   made/Was part of the Roof of Alloway Kirk" and six
   lines from Robert Burns's "Tam O'Shanter" on rim
H. 1¼"; Diam. at rim 2⅜"; L. over handles 3⅜"

John A. Hyman Collection, 1991-596

63. William Law II
Edinburgh, ca. 1700

Law's mark at rim
H. 1"; Diam. at rim 2⅞"; L. over handles 4½"
Wgt. 1 oz. 13 dwt.

John A. Hyman Collection, 1991-116

Clockwise from left: *No. 60. Unmarked quaich, ca. 1750. No. 61. Unmarked quaich, bowl ca. 1700. No. 62. Quaich by Peter Aitken. No. 63. Quaich by William Law II.*

If ever a simple drinking vessel epitomizes a love of country, a deep sense of rootedness, or patriotism, it is the quaich. It speaks so powerfully, whether lamenting the never-to-be-king Bonnie Prince Charlie or recalling a Scottish church for a Scot in far-off Jamaica. What other vessels are so symbolic of a national ethos?

The name "quaich" derives from the Gaelic *cuach,* or cup, and describes a highland bowl form (originally of wood) that became popular in Scotland during the seventeenth century. Some early quaichs were made like barrels, with wooden staves hooped together by bands of willow. Others were turned from single blocks of wood. A rare few have three handles.

These treen examples illustrate both construction methods. The largest, handsomely staved in contrasting woods, is undatable; its bowl may have been made as early as 1700 or as late as 1740, with the rather mechanical silver mounts made and rivetted into place even later. The slight separation between the staves resulted from the wood's shrinking as it dried out over time. This problem may have been exacerbated by someone trying to fit the wood into the mounts by inserting a sharp knife between the staves so they could be compressed. The mounts, though less fluid and plainer than most on mounted quaichs, are unusually complete, encompassing foot ring, girdle, and rim.

Detail of no. 60.

Detail of no. 61.

The next largest treen example can be dated to the mid-seventeenth century from its motto, a clear expression of sympathy for the Scottish uprising under Bonnie Prince Charlie. Like the Aitken piece, it was turned from a single piece of wood.

The silver quaich followed its treen antecedents late in the seventeenth century, converting their functional elements (staves, hoops, lug handles) into pure decoration. Whether in silver or wood, the quaich is circumscribed by convention. For example, the strawberry leaf engraving is characteristic of most quaichs, whether silver mounted or entirely in silver and regardless of period. Despite such limitations, the quaich can be simple or complex, formal or casual, assured or crude, as small as this silver example or as large as eight or more inches in diameter.

The silver quaich was a prized personal possession. According to Ian Finlay, "This type of vessel was held in particular regard and had a special significance in Scottish social ritual. . . . Men no doubt carried small quaichs in their pockets as they carried knives, spoons and snuff-boxes" (*Scottish Gold and Silver Work,* p. 120).

Colin Kirkpatrick of the National Trust for Scotland writes that Ayr was a busy seaport on Scotland's west coast and that many sea masters gave souvenirs for services rendered. A quaich was an ideal gift when made from the timber of the fifteenth-century Alloway Kirk, which, "as you will have read in 'Tam O'Shanter', was a ruin in [Robert] Burns day but had the roof nearly intact until the turn of that century. (18th–19th). The rafters and other load bearing beams were ideal for souvenir makers" (letter, Nov. 19, 1991).

The engraved verse is from Burns's poem "Tam O'Shanter":

"When e'er to drink you are inclined,
Or cutty sarks run through your mind
Think ye may buy the joys o'er dear
Remember Tam O'Shanter's mare"
"He screw'd the pipes and gart them skirl
Till roof and rafters a'did dirl"

Finlay illustrates a number of treen and silver quaichs, in particular two large silver examples engraved with Tudor roses and Jacobite thistles alternating with House of Orange tulips, a political-ly inspired decorative scheme derived from the tumultuous and uncertain times when survival depended on one's loyalties, and one's loyalties depended on a keen sense of the political winds (*Scottish Gold and Silver Work*, pls. 45–47).

In *Treen and Other Wooden Bygones* (London, 1969), Edward H. Pinto illustrates a staved quaich with mounts similar to the one shown here as well as a number of willow-hooped quaichs and the closely related "bickers" and "cogs" (pl. 46).

The unmarked MacDonald quaich is illustrat-ed in Clayton, *Christie's Pictorial History* (p. 228), and in Christie's Glasgow sale catalog of the David Morris Collection, July 3, 1984.

Detail of no. 62.

64–66

THREE EARLY BEAKERS

64. Thomas Dare, Jr.
Taunton, England, ca. 1670

Dare's mark four times, Taunton town mark beneath base
Contemporary pricked inscription "CF to WT Bapt: Febr:
27th: 1646" at rim
H. 3½"; Diam. at rim 3⅛"
Wgt. 3 oz. 2 dwt.

Formerly in the collections of Sir John Wells, M.P., and
David Morris, John A. Hyman Collection, 1991-165

65. Unidentified mark of a black letter "b"
London, 1601/02

Fully marked beneath base
Contemporary engraved initials "R C" beneath base
H. 5¹⁵⁄₁₆"; Diam. at rim 3½"
Wgt. 8 oz. 4 dwt.

Formerly in the collections of Sir Samuel Montagu (Lord
Swaythling) and William Randolph Hearst, 1938-26

66. Unidentified mark of "R" above a cinque-foil
London, 1674/75

Fully marked on bottom
Contemporary engraved inscription "Richard and Katherine
Killingley of Doddington in ye Isle of Ely, Cambridge
Shire" and unidentified armorial on body; contemporary
engraved inscriptions "1674" and "Ann Skeles," later
engraved inscription "I. Neal," and crest (probably for
Pawson, County York) on bottom
H. 3¼"; Diam. at rim 2½"
Wgt. 3 oz. 8 dwt.

John A. Hyman Collection, 1991-140

*No. 64. Beaker by Thomas Dare, Jr. (left). No. 65. Beaker by "b"
(center). No. 66. Beaker by "R" (right).*

As seen on the tallest of these examples, early seventeenth-century English beakers imitated Continental forms in their tall bodies, spread rims, and broad feet. The fact that English beakers were household vessels and that Continental beakers also served as religious plate accounts for differences between the forms.

The tall example is typical of the earliest English beakers in both size and shape, but the engraved design of interlaced strapwork and pendant foliage is more complex than usual. The midband both fills a visual void and frames the design.

By mid-century, beakers had settled at a shorter height, usually less than four inches, that was suited to individual use. Shapes and decorative schemes continued to express Continental origins, but the form's spread foot was reduced to a molded ring because there was no need to compensate for top-heaviness.

Late seventeenth-century English beakers appear in two distinct styles: either engraved in a fashion reminiscent of earlier seventeenth-century tradition or chased in the high relief that became popular after the Restoration (see nos. 19 and 20). The Dare beaker is a splendid example of the later style, rich with full, ripe flowers and leaves subtly offset by shallow vines in a more complex pattern than is usually seen on smaller forms.

The small London "R" beaker is straightforward, its uniqueness stemming from its very English armorial and engraved inscription. Referring to this beaker, Michael Clayton comments, "Only occasionally did owners have proprietary inscriptions engraved on their property" (*Christie's Pictorial History*, p. 73). The inscription is contemporary despite its early date; perhaps belated acknowledgment of a christening by a godfather who fled into exile after the Battle of Naseby in 1645 and returned to England with the Restoration in 1660.

The tall beaker of 1601/2 is illustrated with additional references in Davis, *English Silver at Colonial Williamsburg* (pp. 49–50). The Dare beaker is illustrated in Sotheby's London sale catalog of October 17, 1963, in Clayton, *Collector's Dictionary* (p. 31), and in T. A. Kent's article on the Dare family of Taunton. Kent notes that spoons are the principal surviving form of Taunton silver, and that Taunton cups and beakers are extremely rare ("When Goldsmiths Dare . . . The Story of a Taunton Family," Silver Society *Proceedings*, III [1983], pp. 82–87). The small London "R" beaker is illustrated in Christie's London sale catalog of November 29, 1961, and in Clayton, *Christie's Pictorial History* (p. 73).

67

TRAVEL BEAKER AND SPICE BOX

Probably Thomas Tysoe
London, ca. 1685

Tysoe's mark inside bottom of spice box
Silver gilt
Contemporary engraved arms of Banks impaling Dethick
 for Sir John Banks, first and last baronet of London, and
 his wife, Elizabeth, daughter of Sir John Dethick, lord
 mayor of London
Beaker: H. 3¼"; W. at rim 3¼" x 3⅛"
Wgt. 3 oz. 16 dwt.
Spice Box: H. ⅜"; L. 2¾"; W. 1⅜"
Wgt. 1 oz. 10 dwt.

1976-68, 1 & 2

This wonderfully engraved beaker and spice box were most likely part of a travel canteen similar to another Tysoe example (no. 68) in the collection. They would have been carried in a leather or shagreen case fitted with a wooden plug to hold the various utensils in place. Of the few beakers that have survived from the late seventeenth century, this one is exceptional because of the way the smith has adapted the design—fluid arabesques of vines, leaves, fruits, and bird heads anchored by a pair of glum female terms and surrounding a serious putto trimming a topiary—to such a small area. (The putti decorating each compartment of the spice box appear more relaxed.) The armorial also distinguishes the piece: large cartouches with full armorials are rare on beakers of this period. With matching armorials on the spice box, this pair may be unique.

The oval beaker with its compartmented spice box represents a form popular during the brief period around 1680 to 1690. The shape is linked to a very limited number of makers: Thomas Tysoe, Charles Overing, and the maker known as "FS/S." The three smiths may have worked together. It is known that Overing made the beaker and spice box

No. 67. Spice box (left) *and beaker* (right) *by Thomas Tysoe.*

and that Tysoe made the flatware in a canteen now at the Metropolitan Museum of Art (Hackenbroch, *Silver in the Untermyer Collection*, pl. 95).

To describe the box in terms of probable function masks our uncertainty as to its actual purpose. Harold Newman believes it may have held salt and pepper (*Illustrated Dictionary of Silver*, p. 295). Lou Powers of Colonial Williamsburg's research department favors peppercorns and allspice, both popular during the period. She eliminates salt because it would have corroded the interior (many spice boxes were not protectively gilded) and nutmegs because the compartments are too shallow.

Sir John Banks was created baronet of London in August 1661, shortly after Charles II ascended the throne. Banks died without an heir around 1699 and the title expired with him (John Burke and John Bernard Burke, *A Genealogical and Heraldic History of the Extinct and Dormant Baronetcies of England, Ireland, and Scotland*, 2d ed. [London, 1841; reprint, Baltimore, Md., 1977], p. 35).

Illustrated in Sotheby's London sale catalog of November 27, 1975, in Brett, *Sotheby's Directory of Silver* (p. 142), and in Butler and Walkling, *Book of Wine Antiques* (p. 241).

Other Tysoe/Overing and FS/S canteens are illustrated in Oman, *English Silversmiths' Work Civil and Domestic* (pls. 91–92), and in Brett, *Sotheby's Directory of Silver* (pp. 142–143). The similarities of size and shape are remarkable. The travel canteen at the Metropolitan Museum of Art follows the same form but, in a striking departure from conventional ornament, the beaker is encircled with scenes from a boar hunt.

Detail of beaker.

Detail of spice box.

TWO TRAVEL CANTEENS

No. 68. Travel canteen by Thomas Tysoe.

68. Probably Thomas Tysoe
London, ca. 1690

Beaker and knife unmarked; Tysoe's mark inside each
    compartment of spice box, on heel of spoon, and on tines
    of fork
Beaker: H. 3½"; W. at rim 3½" x 2⅞"
Wgt. 4 oz. 15 dwt.
Spice box: H. ½"; L. 2⅝"; W. 1⅜"
Wgt. 1 oz. 12 dwt.
Spoon: L. 7⅜"
Wgt. 1 oz. 15 dwt.
Fork: L. 6½"
Wgt. 19 dwt.
Knife: L. 7⅛"
Wgt. (with steel/iron blade) 1 oz. 7 dwt.

Formerly in the collection of the British Rail Pension Fund,
    John A. Hyman Collection, 1988-128, 1-5

In style and size, this beaker and spice box are
much like the previous pair (no. 67). When combined with fork, spoon, and knife, they make up a
typical travel canteen of the late seventeenth century. There are few variations in travel canteen equipment: the conventional spoon might be replaced
with a marrow spoon or, early in the next century,
be complemented by a small marrow scoop.

Tysoe has employed the same tight arabesques
and the same bands of overlapping leaves that he
used on the earlier beaker (see no. 67), but here his
figures are lighthearted and personal. What is the
meaning of the young man holding the heart? How
does he relate to the cupid smoking a churchwar-
den (a long-stemmed pipe)? The double spice box
is unusually ornate, with a pair of cupids climbing
the vines on the covers and two aggressive birds
challenging each other through the vines on the
bottoms.

The cannon handles unscrew from the knife, fork, and spoon. The fork and spoon are identical in ornament and form; the knife lacks the round turnings used with the other utensils, probably to maintain a compatible length. Oddly, the handles are not interchangeable.

Reverse of beaker.

Reverse of spice box.

69. Aymé Videau, "D F," and "R P" London, 1746/47

Videau beaker fully marked on bottom; nutmeg grater/ corkscrew marked "D F," possibly for David Field; spoon, fork, and knife marked "R P" on handles; marrow scoop and condiment jar cover unmarked

With original shagreen case with green silk velvet lining and original wooden plug with green silk velvet cover

Beaker: H. 3½"; W. at rim 3½" x 2¾"

Wgt. 4 oz. 6 dwt.

Spoon: L. 7⅞"

Wgt. 2 oz. 13 dwt.

Fork: L. 7⅝"

Wgt. 2 oz. 8 dwt.

Knife: L. 8 ⅜"

Wgt. (handle only) 1 oz. 7 dwt.

Scoop: L. 5½"

Wgt. 12 dwt.

Nutmeg grater/corkscrew: L. (with steel screw and grater) 3½"

Cap for glass condiment jar: L. 3⅜"

John A. Hyman Collection, 1992-233, 1-9

The most obvious difference between this canteen and the Tysoe examples is the absence of surface decoration. Gone are the lovely engraved arabesques and fanciful figures with their implications of a fête champêtre. They are replaced with an understated decorative scheme that relies on the architecture of each object, manifest in the paneled, foliate, capped flatware handles, extra shaping of the scoop and spoon bowls, and the strongly everted beaker rim.

The contrast between this canteen and earlier ones suggests that seventeenth-century examples may have been used less for hunting or campaigning and more as a sign of one's breeding, to be carried on visits to neighbors or while traveling. Eighteenth-century canteens, however, seem to have had a more practical purpose. James Gib, master of the household to Prince Charles Edward Louis Philip Casimir Stuart, described the most historic teen, brought from France, that consisted of a matching silver fork, knife, and spoon. Charles gave this canteen to Murdoch MacLeod, who was wounded at Culloden and who helped guide the prince between Raasay and Skye in his efforts to avoid capture (*ibid.*, pp. 13–14).

The contrast between the Tysoe and Videau canteens shows how the form became more complicated over time, with a greater number of specialized items. The teaspoon-size marrow scoop was added to the usual tablespoon (sometimes also in marrow scoop form). The nutmeg grater was combined with a corkscrew. Earlier nutmeg graters were separate utensils with their own protective silver cylinders, and corkscrews were not part of canteens much before mid-century. The silver-capped

No. 69. Travel canteen by Aymé Videau, "D F," and "R P."

of all British silver canteens merely in terms of its use and storage: "The Prince's hunting equipage in a shagreen case" (George Dalgleish and Dallas Mechan, *'I Am Come Home': Treasures of Prince Charles Edward Stuart* [n.p., 1985], p. 4). Even so, royal hunting was not rough, solitary foraging.

Despite the rigors of a military campaign, the prince also traveled well. He owned a second can-

Detail of no. 69.

condiment jar replaced the compartmented spice box. This one is glass, probably a replacement. Some canteens provided a silver box for spices. Another by Aymé Videau, made in 1736/37, included a folding ruler, possibly the earliest evidence we have of an interest in portion control.

There were a few double canteens: two sets of beakers and a pair of knives, forks, and spoons with a single nutmeg grater, one container for spices, and one marrow scoop. The knives and spoons in Bonnie Prince Charlie's double canteen not only came apart at the shank but also had removable caps so that the handles could be used for spice storage. Also included was a small, shallow, eared bowl.

The Tysoe beaker and spice box are illustrated in Sotheby's London sale catalogs of February 16, 1978, and November 19, 1987, and were exhibited at the Doncaster Museum and Art Gallery from 1983 to 1987. The Videau canteen pictured here is illustrated in Christie's Chicago sale of wine-related objects, December 12, 1992. The Videau canteen of 1736/37 is illustrated in Christie's New York sale catalog of October 30, 1990.

Detail of no. 69.

70
IRISH BEAKER AND STAND

Edward Workman
Dublin, 1719/20

Beaker fully marked at rim; harp beneath foot
Stand marked with harp and date letter beneath body
Contemporary engraved arms and motto "NOLI IRRITARE
  LEONES" of the Lyons family of Ledestown, County
  Westmeath
Beaker: H. 5"; Diam. at rim 3⅞"
Wgt. 8 oz. 5 dwt.
Stand: H. 2"; Diam. at rim 5⅞"
Wgt. 8 oz. 16 dwt.

John A. Hyman Collection, 1991-128, 1 & 2

A major visual difference between Irish and English vessels is the characteristic Irish outward taper that expands capacity and creates a line of great nobility. Many Irish forms share this shape: sugar bowls, stirrup cups, teacups, and larger vessels (see nos. 113 and 121–124). Irish forms provide the ideal stage for elaborate engraved armorials.

Stands were used in combination with drinking vessels both to give the vessels greater visual importance and to catch liquor if it were spilled. The marriage of stand and (invariably covered) cup dates back to the seventeenth century but had fallen into disuse by the time Workman created this handsome set. This Irish beaker-with-stand, one of very few eighteenth-century sets to survive, is noteworthy because it substitutes a beaker, albeit an imposing one, for the covered cup and pairs it with a stand that, despite superb quality, is on a modest scale.

Advertised by Payne and Co., Oxford, in *The Antique Collector* (LXII [March 1991], p. 78).

Detail of stand.

No. 70. Beaker and stand by Edward Workman.

No. 71. Beaker by Thomas Whipham and Charles Wright (left).
No. 72. Beaker probably by Fuller White (center). *No. 73. Beakers*
by Gabriel Sleath (right).

71–73

VIRGINIA-OWNED BEAKERS

71. Thomas Whipham and Charles Wright
London, 1765/66

Fully marked beneath bottom
Contemporary engraved crest of Cole impaling Wormley;
later (early nineteenth-century) engraved name "J. M.
Galt," for either John Minson Galt I (1744–1808) or John
Minson Galt II (1819–1862), and "Williamsburg" on
bottom
H. 4"; Diam. at rim 3⅛"
Wgt. 6 oz. 11 dwt.

John A. Hyman Collection, 1991-603

72. Probably Fuller White
London, 1752/53 or 1753/54

Fully marked beneath bottom
Contemporary engraved arms of the Randolph family of
Virginia
H. 5"; Diam. at rim 4³⁄₁₆"
Wgt. 7 oz. 17 dwt.

1972-335

73. Gabriel Sleath
London, 1735/36

Fully marked beneath bottom of each
Gilt interiors
Contemporary engraved arms of Gooch impaling Stanton
for William Gooch (1681–1751), lieutenant governor of
Virginia, 1727–1749
H. 3⅞"; Diam. at rim 3⅜"
Total wgt. 15 oz.

1975-68, 1 & 2

These attractive and well-made beakers are
historically significant as evidence of the way prominent Virginia families lived during the mid-eighteenth century. They would have been suitable for
any of the well-to-do Englishmen whom Virginians, whether they were members of the provincial

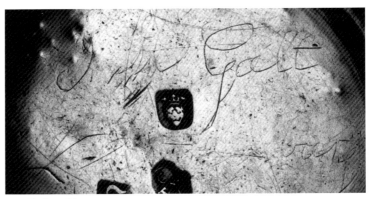

Detail of no. 71.

aristocracy (such as the Randolphs) or well-to-do
traders or professionals (such as the Galts), tried to
emulate. From another perspective, the beakers
show the limited development of this form during
the eighteenth century: details and size vary, but
construction and design remain constant.

John Minson Galt I was senior field surgeon of
the Virginia troops at the end of the War of Indepen-
dence and later attending physician at the Hospital
for the Insane in Williamsburg. The first institution in
America established specifically to deal with mental illness, the hospital has been reconstructed by
Colonial Williamsburg as a museum devoted to
early mental health practices. Galt's grandson, the
physician John Minson Galt II, was also a pioneer
in the treatment of mental health and served as
superintendent at the same institution, later re-
named Eastern State Hospital.

The Randolph and Gooch beakers are illustrat-
ed with provenances and further details in Davis,
English Silver at Williamsburg (pp. 50, 244–245). The
Gooch beakers are also illustrated in Sotheby's
South Africa catalog of March 3, 1975.

No. 74. Beaker by Isaac Cookson.

74
SMALL PROVINCIAL BEAKER

Isaac Cookson
Newcastle upon Tyne, England, ca. 1750

Fully marked beneath base
Contemporary engraved inscription "G*I*D/TO/NELLY"
H. 3½"; Diam. at rim 3"
Wgt. 2 oz. 12 dwt.

John A. Hyman Collection, 1992-129

This provincial beaker has the sharply tapered body, everted rim, and wide-spreading, shaped foot seen most often on Scandinavian examples. This similarity to foreign forms is logical: the seaport of Newcastle upon Tyne had close ties to Scandinavia and the Baltic States. This beaker is more modest in decoration, size, and scale than Scandinavian models. Doesn't its sweetly domestic inscription (so different from the armorials on previous examples) make you ask: who was Nelly?

R. W. Lightbown's *Catalogue of Scandinavian and Baltic Silver* (London, 1975) includes a number of eighteenth-century Swedish beakers related to this example.

75–76
NEOCLASSICAL BEAKERS

75. Probably John Harris III
London, 1788/89

Fully marked at rim
Contemporary engraved cipher "S L"
H. 3⅞"; Diam. at rim 3⅛"
Wgt. 4 oz. 18 dwt.

John A. Hyman Collection, 1991-151

76. Thomas Balliston
London, 1818/19

Fully marked at rim
Parcel gilt exteriors, fully gilt interiors
H. 3½"; Diam. at rim 3¹⁄₁₆"
Total wgt. 9 oz.

John A. Hyman Collection, 1991-455, 1 & 2

No. 75. Beaker probably by John Harris III (left). No. 76. Beakers by Thomas Balliston (right).

These beakers are among the more decorative neoclassical examples of the form. They show little change in shape or size from earlier, plainer versions, except that the usual foot ring is replaced with an engraved band of running leaves on the Balliston pair.

The Balliston beakers are singularly upscale in their reflection of French design, manifest in the wide and richly ornamented band, the four plaques (each with a different putto), and the play of colors and textures in the flat gilt surface against the decorated silver surface. Although such elaborate decorative schemes appeared a decade earlier, they were usually applied to objects such as wine goblets and claret jugs, which were made to be seen by one's guests, rather than to less ceremonial forms such as beakers. This pair also illustrates new technology pioneered by the silver-plating industry. It was no longer necessary to build a body by laboriously hammering it out from a silver ingot. Instead, the smith used a sheet of rolled silver bought on the open market ready to be formed and seamed, a technique made possible by the development of new, smoothly flowing solders.

By comparison, the Harris example seems unexceptional. It is, however, aesthetically important as one of the few beakers decorated with an early neoclassical engraved design.

The Balliston beakers are illustrated in Christie's London catalog of July 10, 1991. Colonial Williamsburg's collection includes a number of secondary examples that are not illustrated in this catalog, such as a circa 1795 Philadelphia beaker by Joseph Lownes.

77–79
THREE SETS OF GOBLETS

77. Henry Hayens
London, 1771/72

Fully marked on face of foot
Gilt interiors
H. 5⅜", 5½"; Diam. at rim 3¹⁵⁄₁₆"
Total wgt. 30 oz. 14 dwt.

1954-553, 1 & 2

Though the goblet is usually seen as distinct from the beaker, transitional examples such as these fall between the two forms. In fact, the goblet is physically no more than a beaker elevated in height and visibility by the addition of a foot and stem, and it serves the same purpose. Beakers and goblets are psychologically separate, however; the added height imparts status to the goblet and permits greater leeway in decoration.

No. 77. Goblets by Henry Hayens.

The relationship between goblet and beaker is the history of design. New forms supplant older ones when the latter are no longer perceived as serving the psychological or stylistic needs of their users, even though both forms serve the same purpose. As eighteenth-century culture progressed, psychological values outstripped physical needs, with new forms developing on the ashes of the old with increasing velocity. The evolution of the goblet, a beaker raised to greater visual consequence, was inevitable.

This pair is especially Augustan, with highly dimensional, applied neoclassical acanthus leaves, tied reeds, and heavy beadwork. Later neoclassical goblets are comparatively featureless, with superficial engraved decoration on a simplified body, and lack the strength and coherence of this remarkable design.

In 1780/81, nine years after this pair was made, Andrew Fogelberg and Stephen Gilbert created a set of six silver-gilt goblets and two ewers following the same proportions and using the same decorative elements (with the addition of medallions depicting Greek mythological figures) as the Hayens goblets. The set, which James Tassie may have modeled, displayed the most fashionable taste of this most fashionable period. Josiah Wedgwood also used Tassie medallions on his basalt ware. He was supplied casts by the popular sculptor John Flaxman, who also created a number of heroic designs for the silversmiths Rundell, Bridge and Rundell. The Fogelberg/Gilbert set is illustrated in the catalog *Gold and Silver from the Al-Tajir Collection* (p. 145).

78. Elizabeth Godfrey
London, 1765/66

Fully marked beneath bodies
Silver gilt
Contemporary engraved arms of a single woman from
    either the Byard, Gates, Chidelly, or Chudleigh family
H. 4¼"; Diam. at rim 3⅛"
Total wgt. 11 oz. 15 dwt.

John A. Hyman Collection, 1991-630, 1 & 2

In their reflection of Huguenot design, these handsome Godfrey goblets provide a visual contrast to the Hayens examples. The Godfrey pieces show how two distinct orientations could successfully coexist during a period when English design was making the transition from the once-predominant rococo style to the rediscovered classic world. These rich and strongly proportioned vessels acknowledge the trend to classicism in their early use

No. 78. Goblets by Elizabeth Godfrey.

of the campana shape, a specifically classical form. In contrast, the swirling gadroons are strongly baroque, though simplified to accommodate the new type of body, and the cartouche and crest are purest rococo.

When compared to the Whipham and Wright beaker made in the same year (see no. 71), this footed pair illustrates the difference between vessels serving the same purpose but made for clients of different social levels. This pair was undoubtedly produced for a custom order placed by a wealthy, fashion-oriented client; the Whipham and Wright beaker was probably selected from a group of standard patterns by someone of more conservative taste. Elizabeth Godfrey catered to the former group; her trade card boasted of patronage by His Royal Highness the Duke of Cumberland, son of George III. Whipham and Wright, to judge from their surviving work, had a well-to-do but less upscale clientele.

79. J. W. Story and William Elliott
London, 1813/14

Fully marked on body
Contemporary unidentified engraved crest, armorial, and
    motto "From the Lips to the Heart"
H. two at 6", one at 7"; Diam. at rim two at 4¼", one at 5"
Total wgt. 42 oz.

John A. Hyman Collection, 1991-629, 1-3

This richly ornamented set combines a narrow guilloche belt with a broad band of richly textured cast and chased grape vines applied over a matted ground, an elegant application of this widely employed theme, which was used to great effect during the early nineteenth century as openwork on wine coasters, baskets, and the borders of trays, or as solid decoration on cups, wine coolers, and vessels of every sort.

No. 79. Goblets by J. W. Story and William Elliott.

Why three goblets rather than two, and why graduated heights? Goblets usually survive as matched pairs or large matched sets. They were probably produced in some number for sale in whatever multiple a client might want. Their stock bodies, distinguished from one another by details added according to the skill of the maker, were intended to serve as vehicles for standard decorative variations. The client selected the ornamentation from a variety of upgrades, including many of considerable complexity, such as that seen here, according to his purse. Yet imposing as they are, these highly styled goblets are based on a rather graceless body available from any number of smiths, none of whom, not even the redoubtable Paul Storr, was able to bring it to life.

Regarding the engraving, Gale Glynn, whose research on heraldic matters is reflected throughout this catalog, allows that "the motto is too good to be true, and is probably a private joke or pertains to some unofficial 'club.' . . . I am inclined to think the whole thing is a bit of fun" (letter, Feb. 13, 1991).

The Hayens goblets are illustrated in Davis, *English Silver at Williamsburg* (pp. 50–51). The Godfrey goblets are illustrated in Sotheby's New York sale catalog of October 31, 1991, and in Christie's London sale catalog of February 28, 1973. The Story and Elliott goblets are illustrated in Christie's New York sale catalog of October 30, 1991. For another use of this rich grapevine pattern, see number 140.

80–81
THE GOBLET AS CLICHÉ

80. Peter Gillois
London, 1768/69

Fully marked at rim
Gilt interiors
Unidentified contemporary engraved crest
H. 4⅞"; Diam. at rim 3½"
Total wgt. 12 oz. 2 dwt.

John A. Hyman Collection, 1993-102, 1 & 2

81. Charles Aldridge and Henry Green
London, 1770/71

Fully marked at rim
Gilt interiors
Unidentified contemporary engraved crest
H. 6¼"; Diam. at rim 2⅞"
Total wgt. 17 oz. 4 dwt.

John A. Hyman Collection, 1993-59, 1 & 2

No. 80. Goblets by Peter Gillois.

A new form of goblet emerged during the latter part of the eighteenth century, with an egg-shaped bowl and two-piece knopped stem (the knop conceals the joint between the two sections). Conventional on the earliest goblets of the period, these elements were possibly taken from familiar ecclesiastical vessels that had been in existence for centuries or from baluster wine cups, sometimes referred to as goblets (see nos. 8–10). Thus revived, the goblet became the dominant form of personal drinking vessel, quickly developing a more open bowl with greater emphasis on line than these examples show, in keeping with the new neoclassical fashion (see no. 82).

There is a marked difference in character between these two sets of early goblets, despite their obvious similarities. The Gillois pair is squat and plain, an invitation to drink. The Aldridge and Green pair is elevated and elegant, an invitation to view. Such differences are not unusual; even within the framework of a highly standardized form, goblets made during the late eighteenth and into the nineteenth century display a considerable range, from utterly unevocative to surprisingly ambitious.

After an absence of more than half a century, why did the goblet suddenly become the vessel of choice for dining table drinking? There is a sense of discontinuity between seventeenth-century goblets,

No. 81. Goblets by Charles Aldridge and Henry Green.

which were primarily ecclesiastical and ceremonial, and these eighteenth-century examples, which served more mundane purposes. This discontinuity is best explained by the great popularity of glass in the interim. First introduced in the late seventeenth century, glass had become a commodity by the middle of the eighteenth century. Since glass was no longer exclusive and was available to virtually all social classes by this time, fashionable dining required new ways to express affluence. What better material than gleaming, expensive silver? What better form than the tall, imposing goblet?

The eighteenth-century goblet has never received the attention it deserves, as is obvious from a survey of most popular texts on silver. With rare exceptions, all but the most brilliant goblets go virtually unacknowledged. Is this because there were so many pedestrian examples that the form is considered banal? Is it because the silver trade is more enamored of ancient, exotic forms? Or is the goblet too close to us in time?

82
BRIGHT-CUT GOBLET

No 82. Goblet by John Emes.

John Emes
London, 1801/02

Fully marked beneath foot
Gilt interior
Slightly later engraved crest and initials "J R"
In original tooled leather case with colored paper and blue
    baize lining bearing the retailer's printed paper label:
    "*RUNDELL and BRIDGE,/Jewellers & Goldsmiths,/To
    their Majesties/No. 32, Ludgate Hill,/London.*"
H. 6½"; Diam. at rim 3⅝"
Wgt. 8 oz. 5 dwt.

John A. Hyman Collection, 1991-628, 1 & 2

Stripped of its wonderful ornament, this is a
conventional goblet, which is akin to saying ham-
burger is another form of filet mignon. The piece is
utterly refined, with a beautifully proportioned
stem that blends foot and body into a coherent,
flowing line. Many goblets of this simple form survive but few, if any, can match the complexity and
elegance of this one's engraving, fluid grace, and
perfect marriage of form and decoration. Though
the decorative motifs are standard for the time,
they were rarely used so extensively: bright-cut
decoration on the foot combined with a reeded foot
ring, a broad engraved band at the apex of the bowl,
plus an additional band encircling its base. The
latter extra bit of decoration was often omitted.

More incredible is the goblet's condition, thanks
to the tooled leather case provided by the retailers
Rundell and Bridge. The engraving, usually worn
because it is surface decoration, is as crisp and visually exciting as the day it was made.

Rundell and Bridge were retailers as well as the royal goldsmiths. They bought many of the goods they retailed from a large network of specialized suppliers that included John Emes; Emes's predecessor, Henry Chawner; and the succeeding firm of Emes and Barnard. The business of Rundell and Bridge started as Theed and Pickett in 1758, then became Pickett and Rundell in 1781 (see the Richmond Racing Cup, no. 136), and Rundell and Bridge in 1788 (Penzer, *Paul Storr*, pp. 69, 71, 72). Through Philip Rundell's single-minded determination to control the silver trade and despite further changes in name and partnership, the firm dominated the highest reaches of the market for many decades as no other firm has before or since.

Illustrated in Sotheby's London sale catalog of November 12, 1991.

Detail of no. 82.

No. 83. Covered mug by "C C."

83

EARLY COVERED MUG

Unidentified mark of "C C" with a tree between and pellets above
London, 1628/29

Fully marked on bottom
Contemporary engraved initials "TEP" for Thomas Penoyre
(1602–1638) on cover and body. By descent to Slade
Penoyre
H. inc. cover 4⅞"; H. of body 3¼"; Diam. at rim 3⅛"
Wgt. 7 oz. 8 dwt.

John A. Hyman Collection, 1993-135

This simple, direct, and handsome mug is a
great rarity in English silver. It is the earliest known
mug and the only example of the form from the
first half of the seventeenth century. It is rare not
merely for its form; it also boasts a known ancestry,
having descended in the Penoyre family until 1986.

In her classic survey of early English silver,
Philippa Glanville lists among the important types

of early English silver drinking vessels mazers,
cups and bowls, tankards and flagons, and beakers
and dram cups. She also refers to a seventeenth-
century form known as a "cann" (Dutch spelling)
or "can." She has described the can as a footless,
beaker-type body with a hinged lid. Smaller than a
tankard, the can was likely to have been a personal
rather than a communal vessel. Glanville notes,
"Taking the terms can, tankard and stoup as identifying a distinctive vessel with similar characteristics, references in inventories are almost always to
one, or at the most, three, by contrast with the sets
or nests of bowls. An inventory of the Bromley family's plate taken in 1628 includes only one can 'with
a cover and barr'd about' (that is a tankard)." She
wonders if the mug shown here might have been
described as a can during the period, even though
its cover is not hinged. (*Silver in Tudor and Early
Stuart England*, pp. 225–277 [quotation on p. 263];
conversation, July 20, 1993.)

Clearly the terms "can" and "tankard" are
booby traps for the present-day researcher. It seems
likely that the mug derived from the tankard, with
which it shared a common function, though perhaps under different social settings.

Visually, this mug is more than the sum of its
parts. It is clearly in the generic form of the tankard, despite the fact that the cover is not hinged to
the body. There is a fine balance between the gently
domed cover and the subtly tapering body as well
as considerable sophistication in the use of a hollow tankard-handle, which has been proportioned
and placed to suit the scale of this body. Handles of
this type are usually associated with status-defin-
ing vessels. In the same way, the ring-handle on the
cover has been adapted from more important objects of the period, such as the Stoke Prior bell salt
of 1596/97 (Glanville, *Silver in Tudor and Early Stuart
England*, p. 461). Of all of the types of available lid

handles, this one is the most functional, allowing the user to slip it over his or her finger to lift and hold the cover while filling or draining the mug.

Before 1986, when this mug first surfaced, it was generally assumed that the mug first became a popular form of vessel during the latter decades of the seventeenth century. As Clayton writes, "Surprisingly, the mug . . . does not appear until the end of the reign of Charles II" (*Collector's Dictionary*, p. 258).

Though the resemblance to the tankard is unmistakable, this body was probably copied from the simplest type of Continental beaker, to which the cover and handle were added. There seems to have been no further development in the shape, and there is no continuity between this body and the later mug form that Clayton mentions (*ibid.*, p. 259).

This mug was unknown until 1986, when it was put up for sale as part of a remarkable and

stylistically consistent group of functional vessels (the group also included two marked porringers and a covered skillet) that were handed down in the same family over three and one-half centuries. Thomas Penoyre of Hay-on-Wye, Herefordshire, the original owner of this mug, descended in a well-settled family whose roots in the area can be traced back to the fifteenth century. A staunch loyalist, he was imprisoned after the defeat of Charles I, accused of having raised soldiers (including his son, James, who at sixteen fought with the Royalists) for the king. Most of Penoyre's lands and possessions were forfeited, but the family recovered them after the Restoration. Thomas Penoyre's lineage continues to the present day.

Illustrated with biographical information in Christie's London sale catalogs of May 21, 1986, and July 14, 1993, and in Schroder, *English Domestic Silver* (p. 104).

Mug with cover removed.

84–88

FIVE EARLY MUGS

84. Unidentified mark of "TO" with a pellet within a circle between
London, 1689/90

Fully marked on bottom
Contemporary chased armorial of Stoughton of Stoke,
    County Surrey, for Nicholas Stoughton (1634–1686);
    contemporary engraved inscription "Ex Dono Nicholas
    Stoughton:in a:gro: Surrey, Ensis Barronetus:" (The Gift
    of Nicholas Stoughton of the county of Surrey, Baronet);
    scratch-engraved initials "W/R R" on bottom
H. 4"; Diam. at rim 3"
Wgt. 7 oz. 4 dwt.

John A. Hyman Collection, 1992-8

No. 84. Mug by "TO."

This is a large example of what may be the earliest popular type of English silver mug. A fair number of examples by several makers survive in highly variable condition (many are lightweight and show signs of heavy use). They were probably made in some quantity.

The reeded neck and handle, taken from Fulham and Nottingham earthenware, are typical, and reflect the shapes and decorations natural to potting technique. In silver, however, the bulbous mug is a dead-end form that lasted a brief period with little variation: the body may be chased in various ways and the handle may be beaded, but little else differs. Such mugs were first seen around 1680 and were soon superseded by straight-sided or baluster forms that lent themselves more easily to the silversmith's hammer.

These chinoiseries are more elaborate than those usually seen on smaller vessels because they include not only the usual exotic birds and shrubs but also two oriental figures: a man and a woman in dramatic poses. The armorial and inscription are particularly rare on mugs, which were intended more for use than display.

Perhaps the most appropriate use of chinoiserie is seen on the rare surviving teabowls of the late seventeenth century. These small footed bowls, sometimes supplied with stands, were copied from the oriental ceramics that were the height of fashion. They were in vogue for a very limited period because they were impractical for hot beverages.

The discrepancy in time between the death of the donor and the date of manufacture suggests that this cup was a bequest made by Sir Nicholas in his will and executed after his death. His remains (along with those of other family members) lie in the Stoughton Chapel at Stoke.

For a rare miniature in this shape, see number 52. For other examples of chinoiserie decoration, see numbers 40 and 41. For a chinoiserie teabowl with stand, see the catalog *50 Years on 57th Street* (pl. 17).

85. John Elston
Exeter, England, 1713/14

Fully marked at rim
Britannia standard
Later engraved initials "GY/DB/1714" on body
H. 3"; Diam. at rim 2¼"
Wgt. 3 oz. 4 dwt.

John A. Hyman Collection, 1991-638

86. John Murch
Plymouth, England, ca. 1695

Murch's mark and "Starling" twice beneath bottom
Contemporary engraved initials "*S*/A*R" beneath bottom
H. 3½"; Diam. at rim 3⅛"
Wgt. 3 oz. 12 dwt.

John A. Hyman Collection, 1991-584

No. 85. Mug by John Elston (left). No. 86. Mug by John Murch (right).

Why are these two rather crude mugs so beguiling? Is it their intimate size? Or their ambiguous apearance? They were created for the same reasons as stylish London silver and the results seem much the same, yet in their provincial interpretation, these mugs are the opposites of tony metropolitan wares.

The Murch mug was based on the bulbous body that was no longer fashionable but has a design scheme of chased flutes and gadroons in the latest style (see no. 48). The Elston mug was based on the straight-sided body that was stylish at the time, but its densely packed, chased decoration had been out of fashion for a decade. Elston applied this tall, reeded foot and bulging gadroons with varying lack of success to a number of small, casual vessels, including the 1701/02 beaker that Tim Kent illustrates in the *Proceedings* of the Silver Society for 1982 (III, p. 56).

These mugs illustrate the ways in which provincial smiths working in secondary centers tried to gratify their clients' demands. Provincial clients were usually one step behind developments in the

city. Thus Murch uses stylish decoration on an obsolete body and Elston uses obsolete decoration on a stylish body.

These examples underscore the way provincial vessels provide a delightful relief from the predictable appearance of sophisticated, London-made prototypes. They are, unfortunately, rare.

The Elston mug is illustrated in Bearne's Torquay sale catalog of November 6, 1991 (a similar Elston example is offered as a separate lot), as well as in *Country Life* (CLXXXV [Nov. 21, 1991], p. 112). Another Elston mug of the same form was formerly in the collection of the marquess of Breadalbane and is illustrated in Jackson, *History of English Plate* (II, p. 773).

No. 87. Mug by John Fawdery I.

87. John Fawdery I
London, 1698/99

Fully marked at rim
Britannia standard
Small later engraved crest opposite handle; contemporary
    engraved initials "C/.I.M." and scratched weight (twice)
    "9"/2" beneath body
H. 3¾"; Diam. at rim 3"
Wgt. 9 oz.

John A. Hyman Collection, 1993-62

The London design of this mug is echoed in
Elston's provincial mug and also links it to the
Sutton example that follows. It boasts more finesse
than the former and more vigorous detail than the
latter, though it may have been seen as old-fashioned at the time. The wide band of tight flutes is
visually cleaner than Elston's bulging gadroons
because the body is less distorted. The use of flutes
accented with punched bands of abstract decoration that offset a molded midband seems more ex-

citing than Sutton's reliance on two sets of molded
bands, but such excitement was on the wane by the
end of the seventeenth century, giving way to a
more tailored look. The cast, beaded handle, a relatively upscale element common to tankards, was
also an obvious design influence for Sutton, who
made a valiant attempt to replicate it using wrought
elements.

The best examples of this period are like this
mug, strong and rhythmic, with a succession of
tightly related, horizontal bands of varying design.
Wark shows a 1700/01 mug by Isaac Dighton that
is equally facile in its use of running belts of highly
decorative punchwork to offset a broad band of
tight fluting (*British Silver in the Huntington Collection*, p. 25).

88. John Sutton
London, 1692/93

Fully marked at rim
Contemporary engraved armorial of a single woman of the
    de La Warr family
H. 4"; Diam. at rim 3⅛"
Wgt. 9 oz. 10 dwt.

John A. Hyman Collection, 1992-83

No. 88. Mug by John Sutton.

This early version of the simple straight-sided mug illustrates a further way in which the English ornamented a utilitarian vessel. Like the Elston and Fawdery examples, it appears rather naive, though it was made with considerable finesse under the umbrella of stylish London design. It also lacks elements such as the cast tankard-type handle seen on the Fawdery mug, which is more typical of good London work.

The reeded bands encircling the body and the beaded rattail handle were typical English ways to create elegance with limited means. These bands, broadly interpreting wooden water-carrying vessels, were used on silver from Elizabethan times. This theme is periodically resurrected. A number of later vessels were based on this stylistic convention (see nos. 126–134), and similar small mugs are made even today. The origins of these bands were still familiar in the seventeenth century. This point of reference has been lost today, yet as pure decoration, the motif is amazingly tenacious, imbedded in the collective subconscious.

The engraved armorial is especially relevant, as the de La Warre family had strong connections with the Virginia tidewater during this period. Maryland, where they were situated, and Virginia were linked through the vast system of waterways that provided the only reliable means of transportation for the entire area, including the large plantations near Williamsburg that were the hubs of commerce.

No. 89. Thistle cup by John Luke, Jr.

89

SCOTTISH THISTLE CUP

John Luke, Jr.
Glasgow, ca. 1700

Luke's mark twice, Glasgow mark, and date letter beneath
  base
Contemporary engraved initials "A S/H G"
H. 3"; Diam. at rim 3¼"
Wgt. 5 oz.

John A. Hyman Collection, 1993-20

During the late seventeenth and early eighteenth centuries, when English artisans were making mugs like numbers 84–88, Scottish smiths danced to their own pipes and produced their own type of mug. Made with an everted rim, the form resembled a thistle in shape and was therefore known as a "thistle cup," an appropriate name, since the thistle is a universal symbol of Scotland.

The thistle form in Scotland never yielded to changes in fashion. It came into being fully developed and remained the same over the ensuing centuries; it is still being made. There are a few variations: the continuous calyx of softly shaped tongues is sometimes omitted, the midband is occasionally doubled, and the conventional strap (seldom cast) handle is sometimes beaded, often not. John Luke's thistle cups are strikingly flared, which may be a Glaswegian characteristic.

The continuously looping calyx encircling the lower body reflects the high-style trend in seventeenth-century London toward applied overlays either cut from flat silver (see no. 43) or cast (nos. 116 and 117). London fashion eventually shifted towards other types of decoration, but the Scottish calyx remained unaltered. It was never, however, very durable because it was worked from thin metal into a hollow shape unsupported by the body. Most thistle cups bear witness in some degree to years of congenial use.

For an Edinburgh-made miniature thistle cup, see number 57. For another example by this smith, dated 1705, see Clayton, *Christie's Pictorial History* (p. 106); for still another John Luke, Jr., example, see Finlay, *Scottish Gold and Silver Work* (pl. 81). Finlay also shows a modestly ornate thistle cup with a beaded foot, midband, and handle (*ibid.*). Commander G. E. P. How illustrates three thistle cups that range in height from about 1½ inches to 3½ inches. The two largest have typical calyxes. The smallest lacks a calyx but is ornamented with a midband, as is a small, straight-sided, Inverness-made mug (*Notes* [Summer 1942], p. 10). Mid-bands are common on Scottish forms and the exception on English mugs.

Left to right: *No. 90. Mug probably by Edward Yorke. No. 91.*
Mug by John East. No. 92. Mug by "IC." No. 93. Mug by Robert
Timbrell and Joseph Bell I.

90–93

FOUR STRAIGHT-SIDED MUGS

90. Probably Edward Yorke
London, 1712/13

Fully marked at rim
Britannia standard
Contemporary engraved arms of Greenway of Rayneforde,
    Oxford, impaling Pierson or Wisbeach, Isle of Ely, and of
    the Counties Bedford and Devon
H. 4½"; Diam. at rim 3½"
Wgt. 16 oz. 1 dwt.

1976-64

91. John East
London, 1705/06

Fully marked at rim; East's mark on handle
Britannia standard
Contemporary engraved inscriptions "In Mem LL" and
    "AD 1712" beneath bottom
H. 4⅞"; Diam. at rim 3⅝"
Wgt. 9 oz. 2 dwt.

Formerly in the collection of the Museum of Fine Arts,
    Boston, 1954-316

92. Unidentified mark of "IC" above a pellet
within a circle
London, 1695/96

Fully marked beneath bottom
Contemporary engraved initials "MI"; later scratched
    weight "8/638" beneath bottom
H. 3"; Diam. at rim 2⅝"
Wgt. 8 oz. 3 dwt.

1963-136

93. Robert Timbrell and Joseph Bell I
London, 1716/17

Fully marked at rim; makers' mark on handle
Britannia standard
Illegible engraved initials beneath bottom
H. 4½"; Diam. at rim 3⅜"
Wgt. 10 oz. 6 dwt.

Formerly in the collection of the Museum of Fine Arts,
    Boston, 1954-315

These four mugs demonstrate the diversity of the objects required to furnish the homes and shops in Colonial Williamsburg's Historic Area. Among other locations, they are displayed in the Golden Ball, the workshop and store of James Craig, an eighteenth-century Williamsburg silversmith. They are also shown in historic houses open to the public, where they are part of the furnishings consonant with each building's size and character, reflecting the economic and social statuses of the owners. Such objects are not intended to meet so-called museum standards regarding singularity, but all are good examples of their form and of the quality (size, weight, workmanship, type of ornament, and condition) most appropriate for reflecting the various levels within colonial society.

The "IC" mug and that by Timbrell and Bell are illustrated in Davis, *English Silver at Williamsburg* (pp. 68–69), where the latter is attributed to Benjamin Bentley rather than Joseph Bell. This error appeared in the second edition of Jackson, *English Goldsmiths and Their Marks* (p. 166), but was corrected in Pickford's 1989 revision (*Jackson's Silver and Gold Marks*, p. 164).

No. 94. Mug by Benjamin Pyne.

94

TRANSITIONAL MUG

Benjamin Pyne
London, 1705/06

Fully marked at rim
Britannia standard
Contemporary unidentified engraved cipher
H. 4½"; Diam. at rim 3¼"
Wgt. 8 oz. 16 dwt.

John A. Hyman Collection, 1992-46

This early form of baluster mug marks a transition from accepted English decoration to Continental style. The English tradition of worked metal shows in the band of swirling gadroons encircling the lower body, but the overall shape is more controlled and refined than either the bulbous or straight-sided types that preceded it (see nos. 84–88 and 90–93). Stripped of all but its architectural elements, the decoration is more sure-handed and needs not the punched decorative bands that characterized vernacular attempts at elegance. In its restrained ornamentation, taut body shape, and use of cast handle, rim, and foot, this mug clearly reflects the Huguenot influence.

Pyne was one of a small group of English smiths who recognized the portents of stylistic change and had both the foresight and technical competence to use them. It is probable, however, that during the transitional period of roughly 1690 to 1710, these enterpreneurs farmed work out to Huguenot smiths or employed them as journeymen in their own shops.

The use of intertwined initials in a graceful mirror cipher, which became popular around the same time as the baluster mug, presents a wonderful marriage of compatible elements based on the play of engraving on surface. Unlike earlier inscriptions and armorials, the cipher is studied rather than spontaneous, disciplined and architectural in the same manner as the mug itself. It represents a step toward the conscious creation of a formal aesthetic. (See also the ciphers on the Fleming tumbler, no. 36, and the Willaume mug, no. 98.) The mirror cipher is still employed by Colonial Williamsburg's silversmiths on jewelry, following designs in Samuel Sympson's *New Book of Ciphers*, published in London circa 1750.

Illustrated in Timothy Schroder's exhibition catalog of October 12–20, 1989.

No. 95. Mug by Paul de Lamerie, 1719/20 (left). No. 96. Mug by Paul de Lamerie, 1734/35 (center). No. 97. Mug by William Ged (right).

95–97

THREE EARLY BALUSTER MUGS

95. Paul de Lamerie
London, 1719/20

Fully marked beneath bottom
Britannia standard
Contemporary engraved arms of Montgomery quartering
    Eglinton (dexter half) and impaling Percy (sinister half);
    engraved weight "10 17" beneath bottom
H. 3¾"; Diam. at rim 3"
Wgt. 10 oz. 12 dwt.

1954-537

96. Paul de Lamerie
London, 1734/35

Fully marked beneath bottom
Later engraved inscription "J R/of Roanoke" for John
    Randolph (1773–1833) over erased engraving
H. 4⅞"; Diam. at rim 3¼"
Wgt. 15 oz. 8 dwt.

1964-434

97. William Ged
Edinburgh, ca. 1710

Fully marked at rim, assay master Edward Penman
Contemporary engraved motto "CURO DUM QUIESCO"
    and arms of Maxwell, Glengaber, Dumfriesshire
H. 4"; Diam. at rim 2⅝"
Wgt. 8 oz. 4 dwt.

John A. Hyman Collection, 1992-47

As an example of controlled grace and elegance, the baluster mug is second to none, even in its first tentative steps toward a doubly curved body. William Ged's rare Scottish example is a remarkably early statement of the baluster form that reminds us how swiftly fashion diffused from the London hub to more sophisticated provincial centers (Edinburgh was more immediately sensitive to London fashion than secondary centers such as Plymouth or Exeter). It shows to great effect a splendid engraved armorial, lies heavily in the hand, is well balanced, and is so successful visually and functionally that few succeeding Scottish mugs developed this shape further.

The later steps that took the baluster form to its ultimate expression are evident in the two simple, elegant Lamerie mugs. The 1734/35 example particularly shows these elements: a fully developed spreading foot, highly developed double-scroll handle, and grinning satyr mask staring straight at the drinker. Is the mask an eighteenth-century pink elephant?

Around the first quarter of the eighteenth century, smaller drinking vessels like these lost much of their significance as statements of fashion. The accoutrements for genteel formal dining and tea ceremonies supplanted silver tumblers, beakers, and mugs as symbols of status and style. Silversmiths devoted their ingenuity and attention to these new wares, which moved to the forefront of innovation and style while more established forms such as the mug stagnated or disappeared from use.

The Lamerie mugs are illustrated with additional references in Davis, *English Silver at Colonial Williamsburg* (pp. 69–70). The 1734/35 mug was included in an exhibition of Paul de Lamerie's work held at Goldsmiths' Hall in London in 1990 and is illustrated in the exhibition catalog *Paul de Lamerie, the Work of England's Master Silversmith* (p. 100). The Ged mug is illustrated in Christie's London sale catalog of March 4, 1992.

Detail of no. 96.

Detail of no. 96.

Left to right: *No. 98. Mug by David Willaume I. No. 99. Mug by John White. No. 100. Miniature mug by John Hugh LeSage. No. 101. Mug by Richard Gurney and Company.*

98–102
FIVE BALUSTER MUGS

98. David Willaume I
London, 1723/24

Fully marked beneath bottom
Britannia standard
Contemporary engraved mirror cipher "R"; scratched
 weight "3-3" beneath bottom
H. 2⅛"; Diam. at rim 1¹³⁄₁₆"
Wgt. 3 oz.

John A. Hyman Collection, 1991-33

99. John White
London, 1752/53

Fully marked beneath base
H. 4⅛"; Diam. at rim 2¹¹⁄₁₆"
Wgt. 8 oz. 4 dwt.

Formerly in the collection of Henry Philip Strause, Richmond, Virginia, 1945-2

100. John Hugh LeSage
London, ca. 1740

LeSage's mark beneath bottom
H. 1⁵⁄₁₆"; Diam. at rim ¹⁵⁄₁₆"
Wgt. 16 dwt.

Gift of Mrs. Milton F. Schaible, 1988-301

101. Richard Gurney and Company
London, 1740/41

Fully marked beneath bottom
Contemporary unidentified engraved armorial
H. 3⅝"; Diam. at rim 2⅝"
Wgt. 6 oz. 10 dwt.

John A. Hyman Collection, 1991-24

The baluster became the standard mug form early in the eighteenth century as a result of the Huguenot-influenced preference for formal, sinuous shapes. The baluster appeared in all forms, particularly the tankard, caster, and jug.

The baluster shape is deceptive: every element (handle, foot, rim treatment, body form) must be compatible and perfectly balanced or the body sags unhappily, the foot flattens, the rim dissipates into thin air, and the handle collides with the body. Some of these problems are hinted at by these four mugs, but, taken as a group, each is more than ordinarily successful.

No alternative mug shapes developed during this extended period of major stylistic change, though other vessels (large cups, tea- and coffee wares, sauceboats, bowls) altered radically. Silver mugs, tankards, and beakers were slowly being replaced by forms in alternate materials, particularly the ceramic cylindrical mug and the wine glass. The new pieces had become relatively inexpensive, so their fragility was no longer a consideration. (A number of footed glass cups remained important commemorative pieces, however.)

These lovely examples show the baluster mug in its many sizes, from LeSage's delightful, rare miniature to John White's full-sized example. They show its development from a barely curving body to a robust, richly swelled shape, from a stodgy C-curve handle to an assured and elegant reversed double scroll that enhances the body's rolling lines. Though small in size, David Willaume's mug must have been a special commission; it is made of expensive Britannia standard three years after the return to sterling, when smiths had the option of using metal of either quality.

Colonial Williamsburg's collection of silver drinking vessels includes several that are not discussed in this catalog. Two such vessels are a baluster mug made in London in 1728/29 by Thomas Tearle and another made by George Boothby in London in 1729/30.

102. Charles Wright
London, 1776/77

Fully marked on bottom
Slightly later engraved inscription "Moulsey Hurst Sepr 1st. 1780," vignette of racing horses, unidentified monogram, and name "Tatler"
H. 5"; Diam. at rim 3⅛"
Wgt. 10 oz.

John A. Hyman Collection, 1992-220

The conversion of domestic silver vessels to racing trophies seems to have taken place over a long period of time. The earliest known example (no. 22) is dated 1666.

Why would anyone part with such a good baluster mug after having enjoyed it for three years? Maybe the sponsor of the race lacked the funds to purchase a newer vessel or had ordered one that wasn't delivered on time. Maybe Tatler's owner had his own mug inscribed to honor the victory.

Moulsey Hurst was a multisport venue just south of the Thames and a stone's throw from Hampton Court Palace. It was especially noted as the site of many of the most important prize fights of the early nineteenth century. The great Regency sports writer, Pierce Egan, has his well-named character Turf comment in *The Pilgrims of the Thames* that "besides racing, coursing &c., most of the principal prize battles have been contested at Moulsey Hurst." One of Isaac Robert Cruikshank's most fascinating works, a panorama designed to be rolled up and carried in one's pocket that measured fourteen feet long by two and one-half inches wide, was called "The Road to a Fight or Going to a Fight at Moulsey-Hurst or A Picture of the Fancy" (J. C. Reid, *Bucks and Bruisers: Pierce Egan and Regency England* [London, 1971], pp. 181 [quotation], 41).

Illustrated in Christie's South Kensington sale catalog of December 1, 1992, where the source of the racing scene is given as James Seymour's engraving of Careless beating Atlas.

No. 102. Mug by Charles Wright.

No. 103. Mug by Adrian Bancker (left). *No. 104. Mug by Adam
Lynn* (center). *No. 105. Mug by Joseph Richardson I* (right).

103–105
THREE AMERICAN MUGS

103. Adrian Bancker
New York City, ca. 1750

Bancker's mark at rim
Contemporary engraved initials "E/R.S" beneath bottom
   for Robert and Elizabeth Schuyler Sanders, daughter of
   Peter Schuyler, the first mayor of Albany. Robert
   Sanders (1705–1765) became Albany's second mayor.
H. 4⅝"; Diam. at rim 3¼"
Wgt. 10 oz. 18 dwt.

Formerly in the Glen-Sanders Collection, Scotia, New York,
   1964-273

104. Adam Lynn
Alexandria, Virginia, 1791–1805

Lynn's mark twice beneath bottom
Contemporary engraved cipher "LB" for Lucy Page
   Burwell (1764–1843), wife of Nathaniel Burwell (1727–
   1799) of Carter's Grove, Williamsburg, and Carter Hall,
   Clarke County, Virginia
H. 5½"; Diam. at rim 3⅜"
Wgt. 15 oz. 18 dwt.

1978-146

105. Joseph Richardson I
Philadelphia, ca. 1735

Richardson's mark at rim on either side of handle
H. 4⅞"; Diam. at rim 3⁵⁄₁₆"
Wgt. 12 oz. 13 dwt.

1953-281

Colonial Williamsburg's collection of silver reflects the fact that until the Revolution, Virginia's upper class emulated English models. Members of the Virginia gentry studied in England, admired English manners, copied English architecture, and, once back in the colony, ordered their luxuries from England. Silver was just one of the things Virginia's wealthier citizens preferred to order from the mother country, even when locally made items of reasonable quality were available. Nonetheless, it is important that Colonial Williamsburg acquire American silver to study the contrasts between imported and domestic forms and between those made in different regions of British North America. Pieces made after 1776 show how much or how little American styles and shapes differed from English models even after the break with England.

As popular in America as it was in England, the baluster mug was made in quantity by American smiths over a long period. The three pictured here are from three centers of silver production and show three distinct degrees of subtlety. The Bancker mug reflects the conservatism of New York design, harkening to earlier, less complex forms such the Willaume mug (no. 98). The Lynn example stands tall and handsome but betrays the lack of an English model on which to base proportion and shape. Only the Richardson mug, the earliest of the three, is comparable to English examples in line and technical mastery.

The Bancker mug is illustrated in Colonial Williamsburg, *Glen-Sanders Collection* (p. 26). The Richardson mug is illustrated in Davis, "The Silver" (*Antiques*, XCV [1969], p. 135).

*No. 109. Tankard by Jacob Gerritse Lansing (left). No. 110.
Tankard by Samuel Casey (center). No. 111. Tankard by
Cornelius Kierstede (right).*

109–111

THREE AMERICAN TANKARDS

109. Jacob Gerritse Lansing
Albany, New York, 1735–1745

Lansing's mark twice at rim
Contemporary engraved initials "D/I*S," for John Sanders (1714–1782) and Deborah Glen (1721–1786), who married in 1739, beneath base. Jacob Gerritse Lansing, maker of this tankard, married Helena Glen, second cousin of Deborah Glen.
H. inc. cover 6⁵⁄₁₆"; Diam. at rim 4⅝"
Wgt. 33 oz. 3 dwt.

Formerly in the Glen-Sanders Collection, Scotia, New York, 1964-271

110. Samuel Casey
South Kingston, Rhode Island, ca. 1765

Casey's mark on bottom
Contemporary engraved initials "D/I*P" on handle; contemporary engraved inscription "John and Priscilea Douglass/Octr 14th 1765" beneath base
H. inc. cover 8½"; Diam. at rim 4⅛"
Wgt. 27 oz. 11 dwt.

1959-253

111. Cornelius Kierstede
New York City, ca. 1720

Kierstede's mark thrice atop cover and twice at rim
Later engraved cipher on cover; later engraved initials "C G" on handle; later engraved initials "EVR" for Elizabeth Van Rensselaer (1771–1778) on body

H. inc. cover 6"; Diam. at rim 4⅝"
Wgt. 33 oz. 9 dwt.

Formerly in the Glen-Sanders Collection, Scotia, New York, 1964-270

These three American tankards illustrate regional diversity in style and technique. Each is typical of the level of taste and silversmithing in its community.

Both the Lansing and Kierstede tankards were "improved" by the addition of spouts during the early nineteenth century, an early implementation of a practice that was widespread later in the century. Two bills for the addition of spouts to silver tankards in the Sanders papers at the New-York Historical Society may well refer to these. The spouts were removed at the time of acquisition by Colonial Williamsburg.

The Lansing and Kierstede tankards are illustrated in Colonial Williamsburg, *Glen-Sanders Collection* (p. 26).

No. 112. Cup probably by Daniel Van Voorhis.

112

SMALL AMERICAN CUP

Probably Daniel Van Voorhis
New York City, ca. 1795

Unmarked
Contemporary engraved cipher "SE" within a bright-cut and pricked cartouche for Sarah Elmendorf, granddaughter of Mary Elmendorf, on body; contemporary engraved inscription "Gift of Mary Elmendorf" (1721–1794) on foot
H. 2⅞"; Diam. at rim 2¹³⁄₁₆"
Wgt. 2 oz. 16 dwt.

Formerly in the Glen-Sanders Collection, Scotia, New York, 1964-278

Engraved in typical New York fashion, this cup is very similar to a Van Voorhis tea caddy in the Waldron Phoenix Belknap, Jr., Collection at the New-York Historical Society. The cup may be included in Van Voorhis's December 21, 1795, bill to Peter Edmund Elmendorf II: "Balance on a Small Cup—£0.19.0" (quoted in Colonial Williamsburg, *Glen-Sanders Collection*, p. 27).
Illustrated *ibid.*

113

LAMBERT CUP

Joseph Walker
Dublin, 1710/11

Harp crowned and date letter on bezel of cover; Walker's mark, harp crowned, date letter, and scratched weight "72,-3" under body
Contemporary engraved crest of Patrick Lambert of Carnagh, County Wexford, who married Catherine White on January 23, 1698, on cover; matching engraved arms on body
H. inc. cover 13⅜"; H. of body 7⅝"; Diam. of body 7½"
Wgt. 71 oz. 15 dwt.

John A. Hyman Collection, 1992-78

Where the sides of the English U-shaped body rise vertically and integrate well with a cover, the sides of the Irish cup expand to an oversized rim unsuited to a cover. The problem is visual: the lines of an Irish cup force the eye to move outward as it moves upward, and the eye naturally resists moving back in for the cover. When Walker's client requested a "covered" cup, he was asking for innovation, a new type of cover that would redirect the viewer's eye in a logical manner without destroying the strength of the Irish body.

Walker's solution was this softly developed ziggurat, made unusually tall to compensate for the breadth of the cup beneath. As befits an immediate (rather than an in-progress) solution, the cover may seem a bit forced but is in fact worked out artfully. It can be studied for its considered architecture or seen casually as a graceful curve. It consists of three quarter rounds, each roughly half the size of the one below and each rising in progressively narrower steps to the dome. The bell-shaped dome faithfully reflects current fashion but is carried to an extreme in order to balance the body.

The quarter round was not new to Irish smiths; it was a routine detail on the feet of Irish

o. 113. Cup by Joseph Walker.

stands and cups (including this one). In its application to new demands resulting from the change to rococo forms, however, the quarter round marks a notable step toward a thought-out philosophy of design. The harp handles, an Irish enthusiasm representative of slightly older London fashion, were important to the success of this design because they move inward to enclose the form. They are a perfect foil for this outwardly expanding type of body, which is probably why they remained in use in Ireland well after they became obsolete in England.

Few early cups express status so overtly. Its towering height, prominent armorials, and harp handles grandly chased with foliage all indicate the cup's function as an object of prestige.

In attempting a stylishly detailed Huguenot form, Walker had to rely on cast elements, rare in Ireland, in new applications. He may have oversized the applied midrib because of inexperience. To compensate, he moved it slightly higher than intended (there are traces of solder used to improve the fit). In turn, he had to move the handles higher, causing the handle plates to overlap the reeded rim and create another fitting problem. The handles of the William Clarke cup (no. 122) made in Cork in 1725/26, present a similar difficulty. In that case, the problem may stem from Clarke's use of available handles too small for the body.

Few known covered cups of the early eighteenth century share this design. Joseph Walker made at least two others: one with the arms of Crofton in 1710/12, and the Masserene Cup in either 1713/14 or 1714/15. Named for Clotworthy, fourth viscount Masserene, the latter is now at the Ulster Museum in Belfast. A William Archdall example is dated 1719/20. Its present whereabouts are unrecorded. An early Dublin covered cup, made by David King in 1707/08, represents a transitional stage between this example and the Bolton covered cup of 1699/1700 (no. 49). It combines the short base, stocky body, and indented lid of the Bolton cup with the later harp handle and upward thrust of this piece (Jackson, *History of English Plate,* I, p. 279).

For a slightly later covered cup with these uniquely Irish proportions, see Davis, *Genius of Irish Silver* (p. 15). The Masserene Cup is illustrated in Bennett, *Irish Georgian Silver* (p. 250). The Crofton cup appears in an S. J. Phillips advertisement in *Apollo: The Magazine of the Arts* (LXXXIII [January 1966], p. xviii). The Archdall cup is illustrated in *The Antique Collector* (XXV [June 1954], p. 121).

114

CUP WITH ENGRAVING ATTRIBUTED TO ELLIS GAMBLE

David Willaume I
London, 1719/20

Contemporary engraved design attributed to the school of
    Ellis Gamble, possibly executed by William Hogarth;
    later engraved cipher "J A B"
H. 5¾"; Diam. at rim 5"
Wgt. 23 oz. 17 dwt.

Formerly in the collection of Eric N. Shrubsole, John A.
    Hyman Collection, 1992-161

Though schooled in a different tradition, the Huguenots seem to have recognized the muscularity inherent in the English U-body cup and retained it virtually unchanged, as this robust example so eloquently attests. The shape is the perfect vehicle for the engraved tour de force that draws so much light to it. Heavy with a rich caulked rim, the bowl

No. 114. Cup by David Willaume I.

rises from a broad, stepped foot, continuing its straight sides to the last moment in order to provide the greatest space for the engraving. The handles match the body in substance, with the ball of the terminal repeated in the uplifted leaf of the cap. Visually, there is no lack, even without the molded midband customary on such bodies: it was probably omitted to create a large surface on which to place the elaborate engraved design. Possibly taken from a French pattern book, the engraving differs dramatically from conventional decorative schemes based on a client's armorial, such as those seen on the cups by Peter Archambo I (nos. 116 and 117) or on more modest examples (see nos. 120–124).

Some ambiguity exists over Hogarth's involvement in the engraving of this cup. Charles Oman argues against it, dating Hogarth's apprenticeship in Gamble's workshop to 1713. According to Oman, Hogarth would have left Gamble to work independently when this cup was made in 1719 or 1720 (*English Engraved Silver*, pp. 91–94). Hogarth, however, began his apprenticeship with Gamble in 1714, serving until about 1720. He was thus Gamble's most experienced engraver in 1719/20.

Certainly Gamble would have entrusted such an important commission to his senior apprentice, whose talents had been proved. Even if Hogarth had left Gamble's shop by 1719 or 1720, he could still have engraved this cup. Hogarth and Gamble appear to have had a continuing relationship. Gamble had Hogarth engrave his trade card, certainly a mark of respect, some years after Hogarth left his employ. Though Hayward dates the trade card to about 1716 (*Huguenot Silver in England*, pl. 95), this date is improbable because Gamble did not move to the location given on the card until 1723 or 1724.

Eric N. Shrubsole has been the dean of American silver dealers for more than five decades. During that period, he has built a highly personal collection that includes many of the finest examples of their kind. He bought this cup from the antiques dealer Ronald A. Lee, who had himself purchased it from the late Thomas Lumley, one of the most perceptive London silver dealers of his generation.

For further information on the relationship between Ellis Gamble and William Hogarth, see Ronald Paulson, *Hogarth: His Life, Art, and Times* (I [New Haven, Conn., 1971], pp. 43–54).

Reverse of no. 114.

No. 115. Cup by Abraham Buteux.

115
LARGE COVERED CUP

Abraham Buteux
London, 1727/28

Leopard's head crowned and date letter on bezel of cover;
    fully marked with lion passant beneath base
Contemporary engraved crest of Adam Cockburn (1656–
    1735), lord Ormiston, of County Haddington (East
    Lothian, Scotland), on cover; Cockburn's contemporary
    engraved arms on body; engraved weight "98=19=0"
    beneath foot
H. inc. cover 13½"; H. of body 8¾"; Diam. at rim 7¼"
Wgt. 98 oz.

John A. Hyman Collection, 1991-599

Made more than a decade after Huguenot smiths adopted the inverted-bell-shaped body, this handsome cup is unusually massive. Other plain examples of this shape are handsome but not this stately; they seldom stand taller than eleven or twelve inches and usually weigh no more than sixty ounces.

John Davis notes that, although the transition between stylistic periods is seldom abrupt, a marked difference exists between Huguenot-inspired forms and those of the earlier Anglo-Dutch genre (conversation, Williamsburg, Va., May 11, 1992). He describes vessels in the Anglo-Dutch tradition as "open" because their worked surfaces expand rather than contain enclosed space. He defines the bell shape as "closed" in the sense that it defines, contains, and controls interior space; it reads volumetrically.

Cups in this form served as proof of an owner's status. Closed and sculptural, they are impressive and obviously expensive. Their splendid balance and strong contour enable them to support complex, overscaled engraved armorials, an elegance of the most meaningful sort that further projects a vessel's importance. The large covered cup was the principal form of display plate during the first half of the eighteenth century. Based on the number surviving, cups such as this one, the Lambert cup (no. 113), and the Brooke and Whichote cups (nos. 116 and 117) appear to have been standard issue for well-to-do men of various social levels.

Abraham Buteux worked from 1719 to 1731. A member of the close-knit second generation of émigré smiths who practiced the Huguenot tradition in England, he specialized in vessels of high quality and sound mainstream design. He married Eliza-beth, the daughter of his godfather, the Huguenot smith Simon Pantin. Elizabeth carried on her husband's business after his death, entering her mark as Elizabeth Buteux. Later she married another smith, Benjamin Godfrey. Upon Godfrey's death in 1741, Elizabeth entered her second mark as Elizabeth Godfrey. She maintained her shop for an additional seventeen years, continuing the Huguenot tradition of fine quality and handsome design (see no. 78) (Grimwade, *London Goldsmiths*, p. 524).

No. 116. Cup by Peter Archambo I, 1738/39 (left). No. 117. Cup by Peter Archambo I, 1732/33 (right).

116–117

TWO COVERED CUPS

116. Peter Archambo I
London, 1738/39

Fully marked on bezel of cover and beneath base
Contemporary engraved crest of the Whichote family of
Aswarby Park, County Lincoln, on cover; contemporary
engraved arms of the Whichote family on body; en-
graved weight "60=5" beneath base
H. inc. cover 10³⁄₁₆"; H. of body 6½"; Diam. at rim 5¾"
Wgt. 59 oz. 13 dwt.

1954-632

117. Peter Archambo I
London, 1732/33

Duty dodger: fully marked beneath base on plate taken
from a smaller piece
Contemporary engraved arms of Brooke of Norton Priory,
County Chester, impaling Wilbraham of Nantwitch for
Sir Thomas Brooke, third baronet, married to Grace,
daughter of Roger Wilbraham of Townsend
H. inc. cover 13"; H. of body 8½"; Diam. at rim 6¾"
Wgt. 88 oz. 10 dwt.

1978-212

The supreme accomplishments of the Huguenot silversmiths stemmed from their ability to su-
perimpose closed Continental discipline on English
shapes in order to embellish them with the Continental decorative schemes they knew so well. The
handle became more complex and sinuous, the
body taller and more disciplined, with greater separation between body, foot, and cover.

Archambo employed a series of French-in-
spired, tightly disciplined, repetitive patterns of
many types, all of which enclosed the body further.
One of the cups shown here is decorated on the
body and the cover with antique masks and intricate, highly dimensional strapwork. The other is
wrapped in alternating foliate overlays, exquisitely
spaced and highlighted against a contrasting matted ground. Despite their prominence, these overlays are only one important design element and are
subordinate to the elaborate engraved armorials
positioned so prominently.

Detail of no. 117.

The inspiration that elevates these masterpieces over lesser examples does not lie in their decorative elements but in the manner in which they are
deployed. Huguenot smiths relied on a family of
identical cast elements, but each smith created his
own conformations. The cast busts on the earlier
Archambo cup are also seen on one by Edward
Feline dated 1734/35. The twisting foliate castings
on the second were used by Paul de Lamerie on a
covered cup dated 1736/37. The handles from the
Lamerie cup appear on one by John LeSage dated
1738/39. This interchangeability of parts provides

for revealing comparison between various Huguenot smiths and is clearly seen in Grimwade, *Rococo Silver* (pl. 3A ff).

"Duty dodgers" such as the 1732/33 cup appeared shortly after 1720 with the return to the sterling standard and the imposition of a tax on new plate of sixpence per ounce. A considerable amount when levied on any large object, the assessment invited evasion. Large cups were easily "dodged" because there was space for a false bottom between the bowl and the foot. Whether at his client's request or not, Archambo presented the assay office with a small vessel (a cream jug or sugar bowl) that was taxed minimally because of its light weight.

After assay, he removed the hallmarked portion and fitted it between the foot and bottom of this larger vessel. This was probably common practice. As Judith Banister notes, the most important smiths, including Archambo, Wickes, and Lamerie, all "dodged" duty at one time or another ("Master of Elegant Silver: Peter Archambo, Free Butcher and Goldsmith," *Country Life*, CLXXIII [1983], p. 1595).

The earlier example is illustrated in Sotheby's London sale catalog of April 29, 1976. The later example is illustrated with additional references in Davis, *English Silver at Williamsburg* (pp. 62–64).

Detail of no. 117.

Detail of no. 117.

118–119

TWO CUPS WITH VIRGINIA HISTORIES

118. Robert Timbrell and Joseph Bell I
London, 1715/16

Fully marked on bezel of cover and on body below rim
Britannia standard
Engraved arms of the Randolph family of Virginia, in which it has descended, contemporary with the later rococo chased decoration and finial
H. inc. cover 10⅝"; H. of body 7¾"; Diam. at rim 5¹³⁄₁₆"
Wgt. 45 oz. 2 dwt.

1942-37

119. Thomas Whipham
London, 1751/52

Fully marked on bezel of cover and beneath base
Unidentified engraved crest on face of cover and within cartouche on body; another set of unidentified engraved arms within cartouche on opposite side of body, contemporary with the later rococo chased decoration and finial. Family tradition of descent in the related Moore, Taylor, Gilliam, and Durfee families. In the mid-nineteenth century, members of the Durfee family lived at Bassett Hall, later the home of Mr. and Mrs. John D. Rockefeller, Jr., and presently one of Colonial Williamsburg's exhibition buildings.
H. inc. cover 12⅛"; H. of body 7⅞"; Diam. at rim 5⅝"
Wgt. 51 oz. 13 dwt.

Gift of the estate of Frances M. Durfey, Leesburg, Virginia, 1990-93

As originally created, these cups were severely plain, like the Buteux example (no. 115). They are valuable evidence of affluent Virginians' willingness to spend the moneys needed to acquire the same kinds of high-style status symbols as the English gentry. They suggest how far Virginians would go to demonstrate not only their social positions but also their Englishness.

Sometime during the nineteenth century, the bodies and covers of these cups were profusely ornamented in the revived rococo style that had become fashionable. Handle faces were flat chased, finials replaced, and updated arms engraved where appropriate. If these aesthetic revisions served to alter these otherwise good cups in unfortunate ways, they are nevertheless important as extremely rare pieces of silver with a documented history of ownership in eighteenth- and nineteenth-century Williamsburg.

The Randolph family cup is illustrated with a complete provenance in Davis, *English Silver at Williamsburg* (pp. 61–62).

No. 118. Cup by Robert Timbrell and Joseph Bell I (left). No. 119.
Cup by Thomas Whipham (right).

No. 120. Cup by Thomas Tearle.

120–123
FOUR TWO-HANDLED CUPS

120. Thomas Tearle
London, 1729/30

Fully marked on body below rim; Tearle's mark on each
  handle
Contemporary engraved initials "U./H·S." on each handle
H. 5⅝"; Diam. at rim 4¾"
Wgt. 16 oz. 10 dwt.

1954-579

121. Joseph Johns
Limerick, Ireland, ca. 1755

John's mark at rim
Contemporary engraved arms, crest, and motto of Single-
  ton impaling Brady for Edward D'Alton Singleton of
  Quinville, County Limerick
H. 5⅛"; Diam. at rim 4⅛"
Wgt. 15 oz. 5 dwt.

John A. Hyman Collection, 1991-597

122. William Clarke of Cork
Dublin, 1725/26

Clarke's mark at rim; Clarke's mark, harp crowned, and
  date letter under body
Contemporary engraved initials "B/C*I" under foot; later
  engraved crest of a member of the Pike family of
  Glendarary, County Mayo, and cipher "EP"; scratched
  weight "34=16" under bottom
H. 7"; Diam. at rim 6⅝"
Wgt. 34 oz.

John A. Hyman Collection, 1991-598

123. Probably Christopher Locker
Dublin, ca. 1750

Locker's mark, Hibernia, and harp crowned at rim
Contemporary engraved arms of Percy Smyth of Head-
  borough, County Waterford; engraved weight "16"3"
  beneath foot
H. 5"; Diam. at rim 3⅞"
Wgt. 16 oz. 1 dwt.

John A. Hyman Collection, 1992-152

Huguenot smiths popularized the inverted-
bell-shaped body and, as seen on preceding illustrations, utilized it as the basis for their grandest
vessels, whose owners used them as symbols of
taste and rank. This body type was also the denom-
inator for an extensive range of lesser forms, such
as these examples from London, Dublin, Limerick,
and Cork.

No. 121. Cup by Joseph Johns (left). No. 122. Cup by William Clarke (center).
No. 123. Cup probably by Christopher Locker (right).

If the four cups pictured here are less grand than their imposing exemplars, that does not mean they were less cherished. Such a cup may have been the largest and most important piece of silver in a merchant's household, lacking a crest only because the owner lacked one. They were also important to the lesser gentry, who craved the most stylish goods available, though they were limited in what they could afford.

The Tearle cup is squarely in the English tradition even as its elevated body and added midband acknowledge Huguenot influence. It retains, however, old-fashioned wrought handles.

How different are the three Irish cups. They use stylish cast elements: the so-called harp handle on the Cork example was a special favorite among the Irish (less so among the English) during the early eighteenth century. In fact, the name "harp handle" is a shorthand way of associating it with Ireland; a crowned harp was the original Dublin hallmark. (On the other hand, "harp handle" seems a rather pallid choice for a handle that so resembles a praying mantis.) In this example, the handle is at its most effective because of the way it towers above the body and turns the eye inward, creating a visual triangle with the base. The triangle is intensified by the thrust of the chased design.

Also Irish is the manner in which the body of Clarke's cup broadens as it rises (see also nos. 70 and 113). Instead of ending in the English everted rim, the sides rise in a majestic taper, amplifying the piece's size without disturbing the balance between body and foot.

The Johns and Locker cups exemplify the very sophisticated Irish approach to rococo design, though they have abandoned the tapered Irish body and have typically Huguenot handles. Where the Johns example is wonderfully simple, the Locker cup represents the rococo in full swing, beginning with the chased and cast band of running foliage on its foot. The Locker cup's cast overlays resemble in concept those on the Archambo cups (nos. 116 and 117), but here they swing off the foot with characteristic Irish vigor. The cast details are virtually identical to the chased designs seen on many other Irish forms of the period, such as cream jugs, baskets, punch strainers, and basting spoons.

A number of important Irish smiths are represented in Colonial Williamsburg's collection of drinking vessels, including provincial smiths whose work is relatively rare. William Clarke was master of the Cork Goldsmiths' Company in 1714/15, and his work usually bears Cork marks, though this cup was sent to Dublin for assay. Joseph Johns was sheriff of Limerick in 1755 and mayor in 1774, indicating his high standing in the community. Joseph Walker (see also no. 59) was master of the Dublin Goldsmith's Company in 1701/02, as was Edward Workman (see no. 70) in 1712/13. John Hamilton (see no. 124) was also master (1714/15) as well as a member of the Common Council of the City of Dublin, serving four terms (1714, 1717, 1723, and 1740). The great Thomas Bolton (see nos. 43 and 49) was not only master in 1692/93 but also lord mayor of Dublin in 1716 (Bennett, *Irish Georgian Silver*, pp. 297, 309).

The Tearle cup is illustrated in Davis, *English Silver at Williamsburg* (pp. 62–63). For other examples of small Irish drinking vessels, see Davis, *Genius of Irish Silver* (p. 16).

Detail of no. 123.

124

LARGE IRISH CUP

John Hamilton
Dublin, 1736/37

Fully marked on body near rim
Contemporary engraved arms of Loftus quartering Loftus,
Hume, and Crewkerne, with Hume quartering others in
pretense for Nicholas, first earl of Ely (d. 1766), who in
1736 married Mary (d. 1740), eldest daughter and heir of
Sir Gustavus Hume, third baronet of Fermough; contem-
porary engraved earl's coronet
H. 8"; Diam. at rim 6¾"
Wgt. 44 oz. 4 dwt.

John A. Hyman Collection, 1993-136

In its general character, this is so clearly an
Irish cup. What can be more typical than the in-
curved harp handles embracing an expanding body
and strongly anchored to a broad foot?

On the other hand, what an exception it is to
other early Irish examples. Most cups based on this
body and handle are content with a crest, inscription, or routine armorials, as shown in Bennett,
Irish Georgian Silver (pp. 84–86), or on the Cork example shown in the preceding illustration (no. 122).
This cup, however, positively sizzles under its decorative scheme: a magnificent, architectural, flat-
chased band of satyr's masks, shells, foliage, and
strapwork set against a matte ground, with an elaborate and exquisitely worked engraved coat of arms
of great refinement set within a brickwork field.
Decoration of this sort appeared briefly in Irish
silver, roughly from 1735 to 1740, before flamboyant and representational, deep-chased, rococo designs soared into popularity.

Though it appears that these intricate, highly
refined decorative elements, which were probably
taken from European pattern books, may be the
work of no more than one or two specialist chasers,

No. 124. Cup by John Hamilton.

such designs appear on pieces by a half-dozen Irish smiths. Of these artisans, Hamilton, Charles Leslie, and Thomas Williamson form a triumvirate of master smiths whose consistency and quality is unsurpassed in any other center. The forms they created included coffeepots, teapots, cream ewers, and, especially, salvers of incomparable elegance. For examples of other forms with this same decoration, see the superb salver by Williamson, 1734/35, and Leslie cream ewer, circa 1740, in Davis, *Genius of Irish Silver* (pp. 27, 31). For another example from John Hamilton's shop, see the coffeepot of 1736/37 in *Folger's Coffee Collection* (p. 29).

Irish cups of this size and shape made during this period were invariably coverless. The few covers that have survived are unrelated to the cups they accompany. This cup was illustrated with a totally inappropriate, unmarked cover in Christie's sale catalog of July 14, 1993.

In addition, though large cups like this one were seldom made in pairs, Hamilton made a second cup identical to this one, clearly for the same client (it bears the same brilliant armorial), that is now in the collection at the Royal Ontario Museum in Toronto, Canada. It dates one year later, 1737/38, but there seems little reason to believe the two were not made as a pair, each assayed when it was ready. Sometime before 1751, the year of his death, Hamilton supplied the second cup with a cover dimensionally chased in the rococo manner. The cover obviously represents an upgrading: covered cups had become more important and stylish, and by 1750 such rococo chasing was the epitome of fashion. Peter Kaellgren, curator at the Royal Ontario Museum, suggests that "even though the cover does not stylistically go with our cup, . . . I believe that the cover was authentically made for it at the time." He continues, "As the same 'master' was responsible for both the cup and the cover, I think that it should be considered a rather important documentary item,—perhaps even the one that documents the demise of the c.1735–1742 Dublin chasing workshop" that decorated the body (letter, Aug. 2, 1993).

Detail of no. 124.

No. 125. Cup by Thomas Whipham and Charles Wright.

125
CORNELYS CUP

Thomas Whipham and Charles Wright
London, 1763/64

Fully marked on bezel of cover and beneath base
Contemporary engraved allegorical figures on each side;
    motto "Through your Uprightness" "The Law has done
    me Justice." on opposite sides above figures; "T:Cornelys/
    1765" beneath figures on one side
H. inc. cover 14⅜"; H. of body 9½"; Diam. at rim 5⅞"
Wgt. 66 oz. 15 dwt.

John A. Hyman Collection, 1990-179. Given to Colonial
    Williamsburg to honor John D. Davis's twenty-fifth
    anniversary as curator of metalwork.

    The great Huguenot smith Paul de Lamerie
escaped from the limitations imposed by the inverted bell shape, replacing it with a gloriously sensual
body that curved from a shapely waist, its arms no
longer akimbo but instead encircling the torso, its
flank flowing fluidly to the foot. Lamerie encrusted
the shape with glorious ornament specific to this
new form. Less compact and less disciplined versions with simplified ornament became the rule for
late rococo silver. The cup pictured here is typical
of the late rococo. Shaped rather like an inverted
pear, it shows smooth separation between the foot
and the body, a steeply rising cover, vigorous handles, and swirling chased decoration. The new shape
was also adapted to many types of vessel, including a tea service that Whipham and Wright provided the Cadwalader family of Philadelphia in 1763/64.
    Theresa Cornelys rose from humble begin-
nings. She was born in Venice in 1723, the daughter
of an actor known only as Imer. By age seventeen
she had become the mistress of Senator Malipiero.
At age thirty, she was the mistress of the margrave
of Bayreuth (through whose influence she became
director of all theaters in the Austrian Netherlands),
though she was married to the dancer Pompeati. In
1759 she lived in Rotterdam with Cornelis de Riger-

boos, whose Christian name she later adopted. She was an intimate friend of Jacques Casanova, who wrote about her richly furnished house in Hammersmith and bragged about being the father of one (the son) of her two children. As a singer using the names Madame Pompeati and Trenty, Cornelys performed on the Continent and in England, including King's Theatre in the Haymarket, London, in 1746.

Her London patron was Elizabeth Chudleigh, the notorious bigamous wife of the second duke of Kingston. In 1760 Theresa Cornelys leased Carlisle House, one of the largest buildings in Soho Square, brilliantly redecorating it as assembly rooms for dancing and card playing, concerts and masquerades. Admission was limited to members of the "Society," which is how subscribers (including the duke of Gloucester, the duke of Buccleuch, David Garrick, the duchess of Northumberland, and Sir Joshua Reynolds) described themselves. Her masquerades drew as many as eight hundred people, with thousands lining the street for a glimpse of the revelers. Of Carlisle House, Fanny Burney wrote, "The magnificence of the rooms, splendour of the illuminations . . . exceeded anything I ever before saw." Horace Walpole commented that Cornelys "made her house a fairy palace for balls, concerts, and masquerades" (*Survey of London*, XXXIII, p. 76).

Carlisle House moved down the social scale as newer and more splendid assembly rooms competed with it. Theresa Cornelys was taken before the magistrates in 1771, the bill of indictment reportedly stating, "That she does keep and maintain a common disorderly house, and did permit and suffer divers loose, idle, and disorderly persons, as well men as women, to be, and remain, during the whole night, rioting, and otherwise misbehaving them-

selves" (*ibid.*, p. 77). As if that wasn't enough, Cornelys was declared bankrupt in the following year and jailed in King's Bench Prison for debts she owed the contractors who had furnished and refurbished Carlisle House. Thomas Chippendale, the cabinetmaker, was one of her creditors and was later accused of diverting her assets for his own benefit (*ibid.*, pp. 77–78; Christopher Gilbert, *The Life and Work of Thomas Chippendale* [New York, 1978], p. 161).

This large cup was undoubtedly engraved to celebrate Cornelys's victory in an action against her in which "she became involved in quarrels, and appears to have been threatened with the terrors of the Alien Act" (*Dictionary of National Biography*, IV [London, 1921–1922], p. 1149). These events appear to have occurred in 1764. The threat was never carried out, and this cup could well have been a gift from Cornelys to a member of the "Society" who influenced the action in her favor.

Charles Wright, in partnership and individually, made in this pattern a number of pieces that have American histories. They include a tea and coffee service that formed part of the dowry of Elizabeth Lloyd of Wye Plantation, Maryland, when she married John Cadwalader of Philadelphia in 1768; part of this service is at the Philadelphia Museum of Art. A similar coffeepot dated 1765/66 is engraved with the arms and crest of Charles Carroll, barrister, and is now at the Maryland Historical Society (Jennifer Faulds Goldsborough, *Silver in Maryland: Catalogue and Exhibition* [Baltimore, Md., (1983?)], p. 231). A plainer coffeepot dated 1763/64, now at Colonial Williamsburg, bears the Carter family crest. Tradition maintains it was owned by Robert Carter (1728–1804) of Williamsburg and Nomini Hall and his descendants.

Detail of no. 125.

Detail of no. 125.

No. 126. Beakers by Samuel Herbert and Company, assembled.

126
PAIR OF FITTED BEAKERS

Samuel Herbert and Company
London, 1767/68

Fully marked on both bottoms
Contemporary engraved inscriptions "Hob" on one beaker, "Nob" on the other
H. (assembled) 4¾"; Diam. at rim 3½"
Total wgt. 14 oz.

John A. Hyman Collection, 1991-453, 1 & 2

The hoop body is especially appropriate for double beakers, which are made so that they assume the shape of a spirits barrel when they are fitted together. This very early double beaker is heavy, compact, and visually more powerful than later examples. The latter are slimmer, taller, more tapered, in an effete proportion at odds with the vigor of the barrel shape.

To "hobnob" is to participate in an English form of manly competition. Two friends get together with matched (so neither can claim unfair advantage) beakers, toasting each other alternately until the bottles are empty and the winner is declared. Was there overtime when hobnobbers' capacities were as well matched as their vessels?

Though most surviving examples of the hooped double beaker date from the late eighteenth and the nineteenth centuries, it is an ancient form. Oman, *English Silver at the Kremlin,* illustrates a magnificent example dated 1572/73 in the Hermitage Museum, Saint Petersburg (pl. 54b).

Detail of no. 126.

No. 127. Tankard by Sebastian and James Crespel (left).
No. 128. Beakers by Henry Chawner (center). No. 129.
Tankard by John Robertson and John Walton (right).

127–129

HOOP-BODY TANKARDS AND BEAKERS

127. Sebastian and James Crespel
London, 1767/68

Fully marked on bottom; the Crespels' mark and lion
    passant beneath cover
Contemporary engraved arms of Haye, County Salop,
    impaling another
H. inc. cover 5"; Diam. at rim 3⅜"
Wgt. 17 oz. 2 dwt.

1954-538

128. Henry Chawner
London, 1790/91

Fully marked on bottom
Gilt interiors
Descended in the Burwell family of Virginia
H. 3⅝"; Diam. at rim 3¼"
Total wgt. 23 oz. 14 dwt.

1980-58, 1 & 2

129. John Robertson and John Walton
Newcastle, England, 1818/19

Fully marked at rim
H. inc. cover 8½"; Diam. at rim 4¾"
Wgt. 31 oz.

Gift of Mrs. Lee J. Spangler, 1972-42

Beakers and tankards are two other popular types of drinking vessels made with hooped bodies. The Crespel tankard is sweetly sized, but why does it lack a thumbpiece to lift the cover for drinking? Is this idiosyncratically Crespel? A set of three Crespel flat-lidded, hoop-body tankards, dated 1765/66 and illustrated in Sotheby's London sale catalog of October 10, 1983, also lack a thumbpiece.

The beakers are part of a group of silver owned by Lucy (1764–1843) and Nathaniel Burwell (1727–1799), early owners of Carter's Grove, now a property of Colonial Williamsburg. An important landowner in the mid-eighteenth century, Burwell served as James City County's representative to the Convention of 1788, where he voted for the adoption of the Constitution of the United States. See number 104 for another Burwell family vessel, a mug belonging to Lucy Burwell.

The Crespel tankard is illustrated in Davis, *English Silver at Williamsburg* (p. 67).

No. 130. Mug by John Parker and Edward Wakelin.

130

NEOCLASSICAL HOOP-BODY MUG

John Parker and Edward Wakelin
London, 1769/70

Fully marked on bottom
Gilt interior
Contemporary engraved crest of Harrington, probably for
    William Stanhope, viscount Petersham, second earl
    (1719–1779); engraved covered cup on either side of
    body; scratched weight "23=13" on bottom
H. 5½"; Diam. at rim 3¾"
Wgt. 23 oz. 12 dwt.

John A. Hyman Collection, 1993-19

Few hoop-body mugs of the late eighteenth century match this one in elegance and strength. Few are so lavishly decorated, not merely with the hoops that identify the style (see nos. 126–129 and 131–134) but also with the addition of simulated staves, alternately matted and sleek, and a gracefully curved body that reflects the design's source, the wooden barrel. The broad reeded handle is a handsome variation that opens to form a shell where it meets the body in an especially felicitous design.

This mug is intended to impress, and not merely with such finely worked, well-considered details. Its size confirms its importance (five and one-half inches tall, holding thirty-five American ounces—compare it to the Emes and Barnard example, no. 132, which holds four), as does its engraved crest and its splendid interior gilding.

Alan Valentine describes William Stanhope as a man "of quite exceptional immorality" who, though he was promoted to general in 1770, "did nothing of great distinction in military affairs and even less in politics" (*The British Establishment, 1760–1784* . . . [Norman, Okla., 1970], p. 817). Stanhope made a suitable marriage to a woman who gave her "whole life up to vanity and folly" (*The Complete Peerage* . . . , VI [London, 1926], p. 326n). Nothing is known about the two covered cups engraved on this mug. The covered cup is a conventional heraldic device, with no specific reference in this instance.

Left to Right: *No. 131. Mug by Sunshing. No. 132. Mug by Rebecca Emes and Edward Barnard I. No. 133. Mug by George Gordon II. No. 134. Mug by Samuel Richards, Jr.*

131–134

FOUR HOOP-BODY MUGS

131. Sunshing
Canton, China, after 1790

Sunshing's mark beneath bottom
H. 2¼"; Diam. at rim 2⅛"
Wgt. 4 oz. 10 dwt.

John A. Hyman Collection, 1991-114

132. Rebecca Emes and Edward Barnard I
London, 1812/13

Fully marked at rim
Gilt interior
Contemporary engraved initials "MHW" on body
H. 2⅜"; Diam. at rim 2"
Wgt. 3 oz.

John A. Hyman Collection, 1991-115

133. George Gordon II
Madras, India, 1803–1833

Gordon's mark beneath bottom
Gilt interior
H. 3¼"; Diam. at rim 2¾"
Wgt. 7 oz. 7 dwt.

John A. Hyman Collection, 1991-113

134. Samuel Richards, Jr.
Philadelphia, ca. 1795

Richard's mark beneath bottom
Contemporary engraved initials "SHC" on body
H. 3¾"; Diam. at rim 2⅝"
Wgt. 8 oz. 5 dwt.

John A. Hyman Collection, 1991-112

In their reference to the hoops that bind a wooden vessel, these four mugs continue a style popular in England as early as Elizabethan times (for a seventeenth-century example, see no. 88). The design converts a major functional element of the simple pail or barrel into a decorative feature, romanticizing a familiar and forthright object. This decorative treatment is seen on many types of vessel—wine coolers, mustard pots, cream pails, beakers—and is as popular in old Sheffield plate as it is in silver. It turns up in other materials, such as redware, pewter, and treen, as well. Conceptually, the hoop body was extremely long lived, reappearing cyclically across the centuries.

The mugs pictured here underscore the close relationship between England and her colonies, where transplanted Englishmen recalled their roots by clinging to remembered styles and objects even after they had gone out of fashion at home. Though made in the same basic form, these pieces vary in proportion and balance, due in part to local tradition, in part to differences in manufacturing methods, and in part to individual memories altered by distance and time. The American and English mugs have hoops incised into the body, whereas the hoops on the Indian and Chinese Export mugs were made separately and then applied. (Some examples are even more literal, with vertical lines that simulate staves.) Where the handle on the Philadelphia example copies the standard English form, the handles on the Indian and English examples show the later addition of the neoclassical detail that was popular in the early nineteenth century.

The Chinese Export example is illustrated in Kernan, *Chait Collection of Chinese Export Silver*, with the comment, "Mugs in this small size are rare" (p. 155).

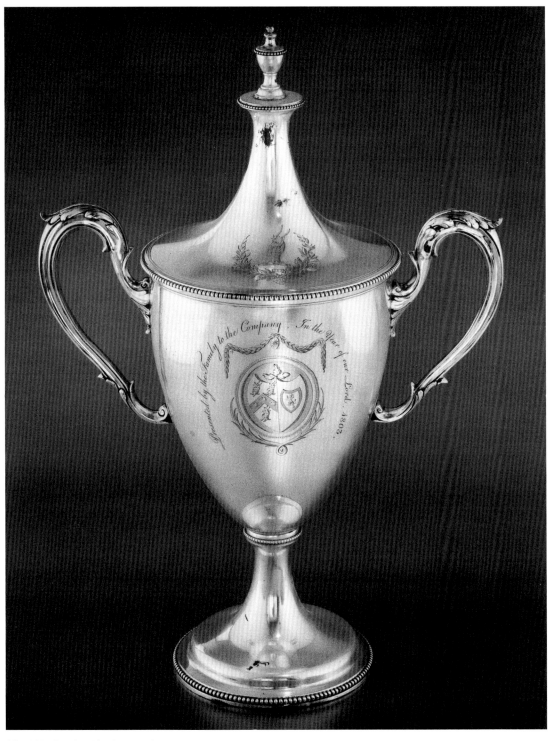

No. 135. Cup by Charles Wright.

135
OYSTER WARS CUP

Charles Wright
London, 1775/76

Fully marked on bezel of cover and beneath base
Contemporary engraved inscription *"The GIFT of the/*Sea
  Salter Co. of Fishermen/*to Thos. Benson Esqr. in consider-
  ation/of his Services on the* Prosecution *of their* Oyster
  Fishery Cause, *wherein a Verdict was/Obtain'd in their
  FAVOUR against the/*TENANTS OF LORD BOLINGBROKE, *on a/
  Special Issue between them, tried at/Maidstone Assizes,
  before/Lord C.J. Mansfield,/the 5 day of August/1772"* within
  an elaborate cartouche on one side of body; later en-
  graved armorial and inscription *"Presented by the Family
  to the Company, In the Year of our Lord, 1803."* on the
  other; "Donors R & I Knock, I. Wright, E. Foreman, Is.
  Tevelain & R Marlborough." on bottom
H. inc. cover 16½"; H. of body 10¾"; Diam. at rim 6½"
Wgt. 64 oz. 11 dwt.

1985-36

Only ten years separate the Oyster Wars Cup
from the Cornelys Cup (no. 125), yet it seems to
come from another world. Neoclassical simplicity
and smoothness have replaced rococo complexity;
only a pair of cast, loop-shaped, foliate handles
suggest what has gone before. The verticality of the
form is exaggerated with an elongated trumpet foot
that is echoed dramatically in the cover, but the
ornament is horizontal, limited to beaded rings at
the foot, body, rim, cover, and finial. The body is
strangely small.

The silver dealer Brand Inglis notes, "It is rare
to find a piece of silver coupling the names of the
important and influential, in this case the great Lord
Chief Justice Mansfield and the Viscount Bolingbroke, with the names of some relatively humble
and probably extremely hard-working fishermen."
Rarer still is a silver object related to a specific legal
matter that can be fully documented. This cup asso-
ciates Lord Chief Justice Mansfield and the vis-

count Bolingbroke with the members of the Sea Salter Company of Fishermen, who went to court to defend their fishing rights against encroachment from the neighboring Faversham Free Fishers, who were under Bolingbroke's protection. Thomas Benson argued the Sea Salter Company's case and won. Members of the company provided him with this cup, which they had inscribed to acknowledge their gratitude. Judging from the second inscription, Benson died some thirty years later and his family generously returned the cup to the fishermen of the Sea Salter Company (information provided by Brand Inglis).

The cup is illustrated in a Brand Inglis advertisement in *The Magazine Antiques* (CXXVI [1984], p. 1358).

Reverse of no. 135.

Detail of no. 135.

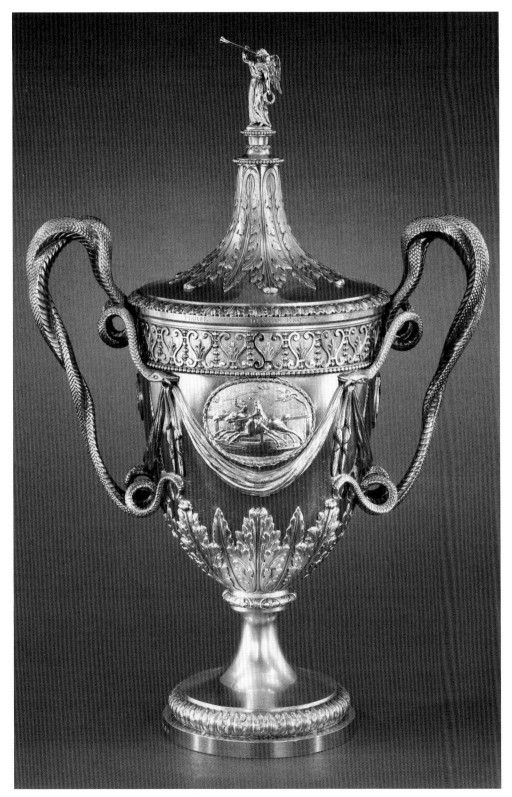

No. 136. Cup by Daniel Smith and Robert Sharp.

136
RICHMOND CUP OF 1776

Daniel Smith and Robert Sharp, under the
auspices of Pickett and Rundell
London, 1776/77

Fully marked on bezel of cover and beneath base
Silver gilt
Contemporary engravings "HENY PIERSE, CHAS. DUNDAS
ESQRS. *STEWARDS 1776*" on one side; "WON BY TUBEROSE."
on the other; "Pickett and Rundell, Fecit.," beneath base.
Pickett and Rundell may have acted as retailers or
arranged the commission.
H. inc. cover 19"; H. of body 11¾"; Diam. at rim 7¼"
Wgt. 131 oz.

1980-205

    Some presentation cups are off-the-shelf mod-
els, modestly conceived and inscribed later to hon-
or a particular event. The Oyster Wars Cup (no.
135) may be such a piece. The grandest presentation cups are gloriously designed and superlatively
crafted and are intended to commemorate one significant event. The series of cups created for the
Richmond Races in the 1760s and 1770s are superi-
or examples of pieces in this category. Made by
Smith and Sharp and supplied by Pickett and Rundell, six of the Richmond cups have survived (from
1764, 1765, 1766, 1768, 1770, and 1776). They consti-
tute a major statement of early neoclassical taste in
English silver. (The most famous designers of this
period, Robert and James Adam, are credited with
the design for the Richmond cups from 1764 and
1770. The original drawing for the cups survives in
the Sir John Soane Museum in London.) They also
provide commentary on the intense competition
between people of rank who prized their racing
victories as symbols of individual merit, verified by
the quality of the trophies they won and the number of equestrian paintings they commissioned.
    Few vessels compare in unabashed preten-
tiousness to the Richmond Cup pictured here. Few

are so handsomely encrusted with thick, complex decoration, and few bear so massively the weight of their period. Yet the Richmond Cup reads as an integrated whole due to its consistency of scale and the stylistic relatedness of its multiple elements. The whole is much more than the sum of its parts.

Certain elements stand out. The intertwined snake handles (a favorite theme from Lamerie's mature masterpieces) are unrivaled until three decades later, when they are echoed in Paul Storr's most elaborate productions. The lyre-motif band at the rim, the calyx of leaves on the body, the rich descending fronds below the allegorical figure of victory, and the wonderfully realistic draperies appear in rich, well-conceived relief. If these details are the clichés of their period, this cup shows how splendidly clichés can be combined to create a decorative tour de force of considerable power. There is passion present, quite unlike the later, impersonal variations of these same motifs, such as the John Scofield cup (no. 139).

The stylish, elaborate cups awarded for the Richmond Races were matched by those produced for numerous other races, among them Doncaster, Newmarket, Nottingham, and Wells. All follow the same overall decorative scheme. Few other silver objects have received such attention; in their glorious riot of fashionable, allegorical ornament, these are prizes well worth the competition.

Tuberose won two virtually identical trophies, the Richmond and Doncaster cups, for two different owners in the same year. (Sir T. Gascoigne bought Tuberose from Sir Thomas Stapleton after her Richmond victory.) Both cups were supplied by Pickett and Rundell (the medallions are slightly changed). Tuberose's Richmond Cup was made by Smith and Sharp and her Doncaster cup by William Holmes, another prominent smith of the period. Pickett probably owned the original drawing and used it to guide potential clients, the choice of smith being incidental (James Lomax, "Heirs to Antiquity: The Lotherton Hall Silver Race Cups," *The Antique Dealer and Collectors Guide*, XLI [1987–1988], p. 30).

Details of no. 136.

137
NEOCLASSICAL COVERED CUP

Charles Wright
London, 1779/80

Fully marked on bezel of cover and beneath base
Gilt interior
Contemporary engraved unidentified crest and earl's
    coronet
H. inc. cover 11¾"; H. of body 8⅜"; Diam. at rim 4⅝"
Wgt. 35 oz. 4 dwt.

John A. Hyman Collection, 1991-28

This elegant cup represents a brief stylistic diversion that appeared between 1770 and 1780. The new body shape was modeled on the egg, whose soft silhouette was enhanced by a series of vertical bands with alternating matted and flat finishes. In one of the rare instances where ceramic design leads and silver design follows (it is usually the other way round), this style is indebted to Josiah Wedgwood's neoclassical basalt ware designs, which employ vertical ribs to lend depth to flat surfaces.

Earlier examples in this style continue a number of rococo embellishments, such as entwined serpent handles and naturalistic finials. Later examples add neoclassical motifs such as swags or urns as secondary elements. On the piece pictured here, an assured neoclassicism is evident in the slender, sweeping handles, urn-shaped finial, beadwork, and festoons of swags. Its intimate size and scale make this example particularly appealing. In contrast, many vessels in this design are enormous: a William Holmes covered cup stands eighteen inches tall and a milk jug stands twelve and one-half inches, larger than many covered cups. The cup is illustrated in Rowe, *Adam Silver* (pl. 22B) and the jug in Brett, *Sotheby's Directory of Silver* (p. 220).

No. 137. Cup by Charles Wright.

For other silver forms in this style, see Rowe, *Adam Silver* (pls. 22A, 22B), and Clayton, *Christie's Pictorial History* (p. 213). Perhaps the best-known example of this style in silver is the tea and coffee service belonging to the great actor David Garrick. Made in 1774 by Orlando Jackson and James Young, it is now at the Victoria and Albert Museum (Brett, *Sotheby's Directory of Silver*, p. 233.) For similar forms from Wedgwood's pottery, see Robin Reilly, *Wedgwood* (I [New York, 1989], p. 406).

138
HENRY DUNCAN CUP

Matthew Boulton and John Fothergill
Birmingham, England, 1778/79

Fully marked on bezel of cover and on base

Later engraved crest, armorial, and motto of Duncan for Adam Duncan (1731–1804), viscount Duncan of Camperdown and baron Duncan of Lundie (Perthshire); contemporary engraved inscription "To/Henry Duncan Esqr./Commdr. of his Majtys. Ship/the Eagle/By whose generous Care/And unremited Attention/The Cargo of the Brig Dolphin/was preserved/When she got aground at the/head of the Elk in 1777/At the Critical time his Britanic/Majtys. Forces were quitting that Place/This Tribute of Gratitude/is most cordially presented/by/the Insurers."

H. to top of handles 12"; H. inc. cover 11⅞"; H. of body 9⅜"; Diam. at rim 6⅛"

Wgt. 64 oz. 5 dwt.

Formerly in the collection of Lady Isla Twisden, John A. Hyman Collection, 1992-4

This extraordinary cup speaks to us on three levels. At its most significant level, it commemorates a

No. 138. Cup by Matthew Boulton and John Fothergill.

major naval activity of the American Revolution, when a massive British fleet of nearly three hundred ships sailed up the Chesapeake Bay. Beginning on August 25, 1777, thirty thousand foot soldiers (the bulk of the British army in North America) disembarked opposite Cecil Court House on the Elk River in preparation for the attack to take Philadelphia. As captain of the fleet under Vice Admiral Viscount Howe, Henry Duncan was responsible for this operation. The *Eagle* was his flagship, and the *Dolphin* may have been a victualler chartered by the crown that ran aground as the fleet began its withdrawal.

On a second level, this is an extremely rare and major example from the early days of Matthew Boulton's Soho Works, the largest and most important silver manufactory in the English Midlands and an innovative force in the Industrial Revolution. There is only one other early cup of this importance identified with Boulton's mark; it was recorded at the Assay Office in 1777/78. The cup pictured here is from the following year and is the only other large cup he recorded during the decade. Boulton, however, presented other objects for assay. Encompassing candlesticks, tureens, jugs, vases, cruet stands, and salts, some of these items share decorative elements with this cup. Boulton was early in his use of interchangeable components.

On a third level, this cup epitomizes high neoclassicism in everything from its form to the type and variety of its decoration: classic female figures within wreaths of flowers, shells, acanthus leaves, fluting tied with bulrushes, and highly dimensional cattail-and-reed handles. Unlike most of his peers, Boulton maintained an in-house design staff. He

also relied on prestigious architects like James Wyatt, who contributed the design for this base, which Boulton also used to good effect on other forms, including a pair of old Sheffield plate candlesticks in the Colonial Williamsburg collection and silver candlesticks exhibited at Goldsmiths' Hall in 1982 (*Boulton and the Toymakers*, fig. 4). Boulton's design books include few large covered cups. The early drawings (from which this cup was taken) are radical for their time, stressing a horizontality quite opposite to the steeply rising lines that constituted a neoclassical convention (see nos. 135, 136, and 139).

Detail of no. 138.

As befits one of the most important works by this brilliant and entrepreneurial silversmith, the Boulton cup made in 1777/78 is illustrated in many books (the existence of this example was unknown to the museum world until the 1990s), in particular Rowe, *Adam Silver* (pl. 52). Rowe also shows the drawing from which the design derived (pl. 53). In concept and form, both the 1777/78 cup and the one shown here are similar, but this cup represents a further development in complexity. The heavily textured, asymmetrical handles are far more dramatic and original than the snake handles employed on the earlier example, and the addition of prominent medallions beneath the handles brings a richness seldom seen, even on the most luxurious display vessels.

No relationship has been found between Captain Henry Duncan, to whom this cup was presented, and Admiral Adam Duncan, whose arms appear on this cup. Adam Duncan was the popular hero whose victory at Camperdown in 1797 prevented a Dutch invasion in aid of the Irish insurgents under Wolfe Tone (John Knox Laughton, ed., *The Naval Miscellany* [London, 1902]). Clearly, the date of the inscription precedes considerably the earliest possible date of the arms, which were not granted until two decades later.

The author is grateful to Mrs. Phyllis Benedikz of the Birmingham Assay Office for her gracious help in tracing this and related pieces of Matthew Boulton silver and to Gordon Bowen-Hassell of the United States Naval Historical Center for sharing the Center's research.

Illustrated in Bearne's (Torquay) sale catalog of November 6, 1991. Reviewed in a number of publications, including *Country Life* (CLXXXV [Nov. 21, 1991], p. 112). Colonial Williamsburg's collections include a number of medals and coins from Boulton's Soho Mint as well as one of his Titus ormolu clocks, and the Lowry Dale Kirby Collection of old Sheffield plate contains a variety of Boulton-made plated wares.

Detail of no. 138.

139

JOHN SCOFIELD COVERED CUP

John Scofield
London, 1786/87

Sovereign's head, lion passant, and Scofield's mark on
    underside of cover; fully marked on foot
H. inc. cover 15¼"; H. of body 10⅛"; Diam. at rim 5¾"
Wgt. 44 oz. 18 dwt.

John A. Hyman Collection, 1990-199

This tall, organized cup is a vision of all that is refined in English neoclassical silver. Using standard motifs, Scofield has created a highly vertical, unyielding form that is compressed visually within a frame created by the handles, its verticality barely relieved by the minimal counter play of horizontal elements. This version of the cool security of neoclassical taste contrasts markedly with the Boulton cup (no. 138). Also a model of neoclassical design, the Boulton cup is stronger and more vigorous due to its expansive body and the complexity of its decorative scheme.

Scofield was one of the preeminent smiths of the late eighteenth century. Arthur Grimwade describes his work in glowing terms: "Scofield displays a high degree of elegant design executed with impeccable craftsmanship, which rivals at best the contemporary French goldsmith Henri Auguste. It was perhaps the restrained taste of the period that prevented Scofield from displaying a virtuosity which might well have given him a reputation equal with Lamerie or Storr." As Grimwade notes, Scofield's name is often spelled "Schofield," but Scofield did not include the h in his signature at Goldsmith's Hall, which we assume was his spelling of choice (*London Goldsmiths*, p. 653).

In *Adam Silver*, Robert Rowe has illustrated a number of superb examples by John Scofield, including candelabra and candlesticks, a soup tureen, cruet frames, and a massive tea urn (pls. 80, 91–96).

No. 139. Cup by John Scofield.

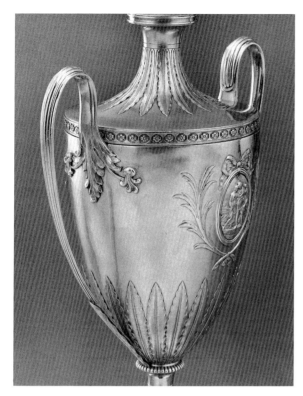

Detail of no. 139.

140
NEOCLASSICAL RACING TROPHY

John Edward Terrey
London, 1816/17

Lion passant on nut holding finial in place; lion passant, date letter, and Terrey's mark on underside of cover; fully marked on body at rim; lion passant and sovereign's head under foot
Gilt interior
Later engraved inscriptions "Won by Eliza beating 15 others" on one side; "Ilsley/1822" on the other
H. inc. cover 11"; H. of body 7½"; Diam. at rim 4¾"
Wgt. 37 oz. 7 dwt.

John A. Hyman Collection, 1991-579

No. 140. Cup by John Edward Terrey.

Racing trophies of this period, so different in sensibility from early examples (see no. 22), tend toward the muscular and the florid, with designs that exemplify whatever is most fashionable. The more important the race, the more exaggerated the trophy.

This trophy is a singular and wonderful exception to that rule. A concession to modesty, it is charming in size and intent and reflects a naturalism that serves as an antidote to the overblown, pseudo-Roman kitsch of the day, despite the grinning Bacchus masks anchoring the handles. Nevertheless, it is clearly intended to be a presentation piece because, despite their sinuous complexity and richness, the cast overlays of grape clusters, grapevines, and grape leaves are carefully parted on both faces to provide space for engraved inscriptions or armorials.

The cast overlays on the foot, rim, and body are beautifully textured by delicate chasing. Supremely realistic, they are unusually airy and dimensional because (unlike similar decoration on most vessels) they are not chased into the body or soldered onto it. They are fastened instead by a series of small nuts within the bowl and below the underside of the foot and cover. It would nice to know if this smith offered a single body with a variety of interchangeable decorative parts in order to offer custom-designed silver based on a limited, easily produced carcass. Though not unusual at this time, bolted components were usually used only for secondary parts rather than an entire set of decoration.

This cup differs substantially from earlier neoclassical vessels in Colonial Williamsburg's collection because it is based on the so-called campana body. This Roman form did not become popular as a model for silver shapes until early in the nineteenth century, when it was frequently adapted for wine coolers, ice buckets, and presentation cups.

Racing cups, first for horse racing, then with yacht racing added during the nineteenth century, have long been important trophies for the nobility, the higher gentry, and those with aspirations to social status. They remain so in our time. Most suffer from the florid excesses characteristic of much nineteenth-century silver, and, though some might be considered handsome, seem overbearing to our contemporary eyes. With few exceptions, both the ugly and the elegant exhibit a self-consciousness that is lacking in this delightful example. For two extraordinary groups of racing trophies from this period, all extremely complex, overloaded with elaborate castings, and richly gilded, see lots 35–39 in Christie's London sale catalog of October 23, 1991, and lots 39–45 in their sale of July 8, 1992. The large number of cups won by Sir Thomas Lipton is displayed at the Glasgow Art Gallery.

Detail of no. 140.

141

PATRIOTIC FUND VASE

Benjamin Smith II under the auspices of
    Rundell, Bridge and Rundell
London, 1807/08

Smith's mark and lion rampant on lion's flank; intaglio
number "2" on lion's paw; Smith's mark, lion rampant,
date letter, and intaglio number "2" on bezel of collar
and bezel of lid; fully marked on side of base

Contemporary engraved inscription *"From the PATRIOTIC
FUND at LLOYDS/TO LAURENCE WILLIAM HALSTED ESQR.
CAPTAIN OF H.M.S. NAMUR./For his MERITORIOUS SERVICES,
in CONTRIBUTING to the DECISIVE VICTORY,/OBTAINED OVER A
SQUADRON OF FRENCH MEN OF WAR, OFF FERROL./on 4th of
November 1805"* on cover; "RUNDELL BRIDGE ET
RUNDELL AURIFICES REGIS ET PRINCIPIS WALLIAE
LONDINI FECERUNT" on side of base

In original chamois-lined, fitted oak case; printed paper
label "RUNDELL, BRIDGE & RUNDELL, Goldsmiths,
Jewellers, Watch Makers, &c, To their Majesties, Their
Royal Highnesses the Prince of Wales, Duke of York,
and Royal Family, Ludgate Hill, London, as well as later
wax seals, shipping labels and the label of Maj.-General
H. C. Money, C.B." within lid. By direct descent through
the family until the present

H. to top of handles 15½"; H. of body 10⅝"; Diam. at rim
7¾"

Wgt. 117 oz. 16 dwt.

John A. Hyman Collection, 1991-643

    The public face of English imperialism is no-
where revealed as clearly as in the series of elaborate formal vases created to reward the success of
individual men fighting the Napoleonic Wars. Lad-
en with highly polarized symbols of British commer-
cial and military power and valued at one hundred
pounds, these awards were given by the Patriotic
Fund that Lloyd's of London had established for
this purpose. Other awards included a ceremonial
sword and a medal. John Shaw designed the cup,
which was later modified by the sculptor John Flax-

No. 141. Cup by Benjamin Smith II.

man. The medal was selected through a design competition. The great majority of these awards went to officers (primarily naval), with Captain Sir E. Berry and Commander Sir H. Popham each honored twice.

Patriotic Fund vases are nearly identical, with only minor changes in decoration. The band of laurel (symbolic of victory) on the neck is sometimes replaced by oak leaves and acorns (symbolic of the oak from which English ships were built). The calyx of English oak sprays with water leaves is occasionally changed to laurel buds and leaves. The symbolism of these alternative motifs is no less charged.

The prowling lion on the cover personifies Britain and remains her symbol to this day. England's mother goddess, a seated Britannia, occupies one side. She holds in her extended right hand the figure of Victory bearing a wreath of laurel, in her left hand a palm branch and a shield bearing the (presumably) English lion. A classical helmet crowns her head, symbolic of Athena, the Greek goddess of wisdom. The other side of the vase shows a powerful warrior in a war helmet, his loose cloak flying off his muscular body, probably Hercules fighting the Lernaean Hydra. The designer leaves no doubt who will win.

The towering handles are hardly ordinary. They are copied from pottery of the classical world, which to the English of the late eighteenth and early nineteenth centuries was the wellspring of artistic and intellectual genius. The simulated cable framing the handles and repeated on the body symbolize the hawsers of British men-of-war. Though they are consonant with the origins of the form, the Greek krater, the handles would be more sympathetic to the overall design were they turned to the outside,

as in Matthew Boulton's ormolu perfume burner at Temple Newsam House (illustrated in Goodison, *Ormolu*, pl. 71). Here, they raise the focal point above even the prowling lion, whom they cage. Heroic excess expressed so bombastically is too serious to succeed.

This is most emphatically a piece of display silver. Based on the unusual cover, which consists

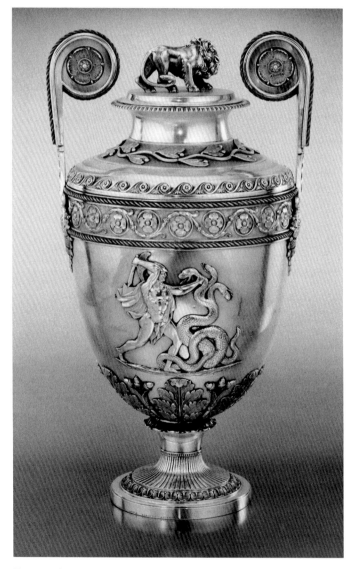

Reverse of no. 141.

of a collar and a lid (the lion finial and its flat plate), it is probable that the Patriotic Fund vase was designed to serve as a wine cooler. Remove the collar and the lid to create an opening large enough to drop in ice and a bottle. Replace the collar for an opening of proper size to hold the bottle upright.

Sixty-eight vases in this form and worth the prescribed one hundred pounds, some enhanced with special plinths at higher cost, were distributed between October 1803 and January 1809. Five additional vases of less grandiose design and lesser value plus a number of swords and medals were also issued. Patriot Fund vases were also awarded for actions in Curaçao, Buenos Aires, San Domingo, Montevideo, and Cuba.

The vase pictured here commemorates the British victory at El Ferrol, one of Spain's three largest ports, in 1805. Located on the country's northwestern coast, El Ferrol boasted a fine natural harbor accessible only through a narrow strait. The British had been defeated there in 1799 but fared better in this engagement, one of a series of battles that preceded Wellington's Peninsula campaigns.

Colonial Williamsburg does not usually collect objects for their grandeur or iconography; they must have some relationship to the colonial experience. This vase is not the exception to this policy that it seems. It is a product of the Anglo-French struggle for economic hegemony in Europe, a struggle that was fought in North America until 1763 and that led to the French alliance with the rebelling colonies. As much as any artifact, this vase strikingly reveals English use of classical images as propaganda to further the Empire's economic goals through military activity in Spain, India, and the Americas. Five

Detail of no. 141.

years after the vase was made, the United States was again embroiled in this contest as it battled Britain in the War of 1812.

Though only sixty-eight recipients are recorded, it seems that Rundell may have ordered extra bodies in anticipation of orders that never came. Sotheby's London sale catalog of June 13, 1974, shows a vase made on the Patriotic Fund model with the same body, foot, handles, and decorative elements, though Hercules is hydra bashing somewhere else and Victory has been turned into an elaborate cast finial with navigational instruments at her feet. Was this vase made from overstock? Unusually, it is credited to three makers: body by Scott and Smith (1806/07), cover by Benjamin Smith

(1807/08), and finial by John Emes (no known date), as usual under the aegis of Rundell, who stamped the base with his customary inscription. Was Rundell stuck with an extra body that he combined with parts from inventory to flog into the market, not wishing to lose the cost of fabrication?

Leslie Southwick has published a splendidly detailed account of the design and history of the Patriotic Fund vases ("The Silver Vases Awarded by the *Patriotic Fund*," *Silver Society Journal* [Winter 1990], pp. 27–49). This vase is illustrated in Sotheby's London sale catalog of November 12, 1991.

Detail of no. 141.

Bibliography

This list includes the books referred to most often in the preparation of this catalog. In addition, sale catalogs published by Sotheby's and Christie's in London and New York have been relied on heavily. They offer an immense diversity of material soundly (if not completely) described. The *Proceedings* of the Silver Society (now known as *The Silver Society Journal*) also have been an invaluable source of information. Among other periodicals, material has come primarily from *Country Life, The Magazine Antiques, Apollo, Antique Collector,* and *Connoisseur.*

GENERAL

Banister, Judith. *An Introduction to Old English Silver.* London: Evans Brothers, 1965.

Bennett, Douglas. *Irish Georgian Silver.* London: Cassell and Company, 1972.

Blair, Claude, ed. *The History of Silver.* London: Macdonald and Company, 1987.

Brett, Vanessa. *The Sotheby's Directory of Silver, 1600–1940.* London: Philip Wilson Publishers for Sotheby's Publications, 1986.

Butler, Robin, and Gillian Walkling. *The Book of Wine Antiques.* Woodbridge, Eng.: Antique Collectors' Club, 1986.

Clayton, Michael. *Christie's Pictorial History of English and American Silver.* Oxford: Phaidon · Christie's Limited, 1985.

————. *The Collector's Dictionary of the Silver and Gold of Great Britain and North America.* 2d ed. Woodbridge, Eng.: Antique Collectors's Club, 1985.

DeLieb, Eric. *Investing in Silver.* London: Transworld Publishers, 1970.

Dennis, Faith. *Three Centuries of French Domestic Silver: Its Makers and Its Marks.* 2 vols. New York: Metropolitan Museum of Art, 1960.

Fales, Martha Gandy. *Early American Silver.* New York: Dutton, 1973.

Finlay, Ian. *Scottish Gold and Silver Work.* Rev. ed., ed. Henry Fothringham. Stevenage, Eng.: Strong Oak Press, 1991.

Forbes, H. A. Crosby, John Devereux Kernan, and Ruth S. Wilkins. *Chinese Export Silver, 1785 to 1885.* Milton, Mass.: Museum of the American China Trade, 1975.

Frederiks, J. W. *Dutch Silver.* 4 vols. The Hague: Martinus Nijhoff, 1952–1961.

[Frégnac, Claude]. *French Master Goldsmiths and Silversmiths from the Seventeenth to the Nineteenth Century.* New York: French & European Publications, 1966.

Glanville, Philippa. *Silver in England.* London: Unwin Hyman, 1987.

Gruber, Alain. *Silverware.* New York: Rizzoli International Publications, 1982.

Holland, Margaret. *Old Country Silver: An Account of English Provincial Silver, with Sections on Ireland, Scotland and Wales.* Newton Abbot, Eng.: David & Charles, 1971.

Honour, Hugh. *Goldsmiths & Silversmiths.* London: Weidenfeld & Nicolson, 1971.

Hood, Graham. *American Silver: A History of Style, 1650–1900.* Rev. ed. New York: E. P. Dutton, 1989.

How, G. E. P. *Notes on Antique Silver (Nos. 1–6 Inclusive) and a Re-Print of Certain Other Published Articles.* Edinburgh: How, [1951].

Jackson, Charles James. *An Illustrated History of English Plate. . . .* 2 vols. London: Country Life and B. T. Batsford, 1911.

Newman, Harold. *An Illustrated Dictionary of Silverware. . . .* London: Thames and Hudson, 1987.

Schroder, Timothy B. *The National Trust Book of English Domestic Silver, 1500–1900.* New York: Viking in association with the National Trust, 1988.

Waldron, Peter. *The Price Guide to Antique Silver.* 2d ed. Woodbridge, Eng.: Antique Collectors' Club, 1982.

COLLECTION AND EXHIBITION CATALOGS

Alcorn, Ellenor. *English Silver in the Museum of Fine Arts, Boston.* Boston: Museum of Fine Arts, 1993.

Birmingham Gold and Silver, 1773–1973. Birmingham, Eng.: City Museum and Art Gallery, 1973.

Buhler, Kathryn C. *American Silver: From the Colonial Period through the Early Republic in the Worcester Art Museum.* Worcester, Mass.: The Museum, 1979.

———. *American Silver, 1655–1825, in the Museum of Fine Arts, Boston.* 2 vols. Boston: Museum of Fine Arts, 1972.

Buhler, Kathryn C., and Graham Hood. *American Silver: Garvan and Other Collections in the Yale University Art Gallery.* 2 vols. New Haven, Conn.: Yale University Press, 1970.

Colonial Williamsburg Foundation. *The Glen-Sanders Collection from Scotia, New York.* Williamsburg, Va.: Colonial Williamsburg Foundation, ca. 1966.

Crighton, R. A., comp. *Cambridge Plate.* . . . Cambridge: Fitzwilliam Museum, 1975.

Dalgleish, George, and Stuart Maxwell. *The Lovable Craft, 1687–1987.* . . . Edinburgh: National Museums of Scotland and the Incorporation of Goldsmiths of the City of Edinburgh, 1987.

Davis, John D. *English Silver at Williamsburg.* Williamsburg, Va.: Colonial Williamsburg Foundation, 1976.

———. *The Genius of Irish Silver: A Texas Private Collection.* Williamsburg, Va.: Colonial Williamsburg Foundation, 1991.

den Blaauwen, A. L., ed. *Dutch Silver, 1580–1830.* Amsterdam: Rijksmuseum, 1979.

50 Years on 57th Street. . . . Ed. Bard Langstaff and James McConnaughy. New York: S. J. Shrubsole Corp., 1986.

Flynt, Henry N., and Martha Gandy Fales. *The Heritage Foundation Collection of Silver.* . . . Deerfield, Mass.: Heritage Foundation, 1968.

The Folger's Coffee Collection of Antique English Silver Coffee Pots and Accessories. Ed. Ross E. Taggard. N.p.: Procter and Gamble Company, n.d.

Glanville, Philippa, and Jennifer Faulds Goldsborough. *Women Silversmiths, 1685–1845: Works from the Collection of the National Museum of Women in the Arts.* New York: Thames and Hudson, 1990.

The Glory of the Goldsmith: Magnificent Gold and Silver from the Al-Tajir Collection. London: Christie's, 1989.

The Goldsmith and the Grape: Silver in the Service of Wine. London: Goldsmiths' Company, 1983.

Hackenbroch, Yvonne. *English and Other Silver in the Irwin Untermyer Collection.* Rev. ed. [New York]: Metropolitan Museum of Art, 1969.

Irish Silver from the Seventeenth to the Nineteenth Century. Washington, D. C.: Smithsonian Institution, 1982.

Jackson-Stops, Gervase, ed. *The Treasure Houses of Britain: Five Hundred Years of Private Patronage and Art Collecting.* Washington, D. C.: National Gallery of Art, 1985.

Kernan, John Devereux. *The Chait Collection of Chinese Export Silver.* New York: Ralph M. Chait Galleries, 1985.

The Lipton Collection: Antique English Silver Designed for the Serving of Tea. Dayton, Ohio: Dayton Art Institute in collaboration with Thomas J. Lipton, Inc., 1958.

Lomax, James. *British Silver at Temple Newsam and Lotherton Hall: A Catalogue of the Leeds Collection.* Leeds, Eng.: Leeds Art Collections Fund, 1992.

Miles, Elizabeth B. *English Silver: Introduction and Catalogue.* Hartford, Conn.: Wadsworth Atheneum, 1976.

Oman, Charles. *The English Silver in the Kremlin, 1557–1663.* London: Methuen & Co., 1961.

Paul de Lamerie: The Work of England's Master Silversmith. London: Goldsmiths' Company, 1990.

Puig, Francis J., Judith Banister, Gerald W. R. Ward, and David McFadden. *English and American Silver in the Collection of the Minneapolis Institute of Arts.* Minneapolis, Minn.: Minneapolis Institute of Arts, 1989.

Ransome-Wallis, Rosemary. *Matthew Boulton and the Toymakers: Silver from the Birmingham Assay Office.* London: Goldsmiths' Company, 1982.

Sassoon, Philip. *A Loan Exhibit of Old English Plate.* London: n.p., 1929.

Schroder, Timothy B. *The Art of the European Goldsmith: Silver from the Schroder Collection.* New York: American Federation of Arts, 1983.

———. *The Gilbert Collection of Gold and Silver.* Los Angeles, Calif.: Los Angeles County Museum of Art, 1988.

Selections from the Campbell Museum Collection. 5th ed. Camden, N. J.: Campbell Museum, 1983.

Southern Silver: An Exhibition of Silver Made in the South Prior to 1860. Houston, Tex.: Museum of Fine Arts, 1968.

Teahan, John. *Irish Silver: A Guide to the Exhibition.* Dublin: Stationery Office, 1979.

Touching Gold & Silver: 500 Years of Hallmarks. London: Goldsmiths' Company, 1978.

Ward, Barbara McLean, and Gerald W. R. Ward, eds. *Silver in American Life: Selections from the Mabel Brady Garvan and Other Collections at Yale University.* N.p.: American Federation of Arts, 1979.

Wark, Robert R. *British Silver in the Huntington Collection.* San Marino, Calif.: Huntington Library, 1978.

Warren, David B., Katherine S. Howe, and Michael K. Brown. *Marks of Achievement: Four Centuries of American Presentation Silver.* Houston, Tex.: Museum of Fine Arts, 1987.

HALLMARKS AND RELATED MATERIAL

Belden, Louise Conway. *Marks of American Silversmiths in the Ineson-Bissell Collection.* Charlottesville, Va.: University Press of Virginia for the Henry Francis du Pont Winterthur Museum, 1980.

Culme, John. *The Directory of Gold and Silversmiths, Jewellers and Allied Traders, 1838–1914 (from the London Assay Office Registers).* 2 vols. Woodbridge, Eng.: Antique Collectors' Club, 1987.

Grimwade, Arthur G. *London Goldsmiths, 1697–1837: Their Marks and Lives. . . .* London: Faber and Faber, 1976.

Heal, Sir Ambrose. *The London Goldsmiths, 1200–1800. . . .* London: Cambridge University Press, 1935.

Jackson, Charles James. *English Goldsmiths and Their Marks. . . .* 2d ed., rev. and enl. New York: Dover Publications, 1964.

Pickford, Ian, ed. *Jackson's Silver and Gold Marks of England, Scotland & Ireland.* 3d ed., rev. Woodbridge, Eng.: Antique Collectors' Club, 1989.

Rainwater, Dorothy T. *American Silver Manufacturers.* Hanover, Pa.: Everybody's Press, 1966.

Wilkinson, Wynyard R. T. *The Makers of Indian Colonial Silver. . . .* London: W. R. T. Wilkinson, 1987.

PERIODS AND STYLES

Culme, John. *Nineteenth-Century Silver.* London: Hamlyn Publishing Group, 1977.

Glanville, Philippa. *Silver in Tudor and Early Stuart England: A Social History and Catalogue of the National Collection, 1480–1660.* London: Victoria and Albert Museum, 1990.

Grimwade, Arthur G. *Rococo Silver, 1727–1765.* London: Faber and Faber, 1974.

Hayward, J. F. *Huguenot Silver in England, 1688–1727.* London: Faber and Faber, 1959.

Houart, Victor. *Miniature Silver Toys.* Trans. David Smith. New York: Alpine Fine Art Books, 1981.

Oman, Charles. *Caroline Silver, 1625–1688.* London: Faber and Faber, 1970.

———. *English Engraved Silver, 1150 to 1900.* London: Faber & Faber, 1978.

———. *English Silversmiths' Work Civil and Domestic: An Introduction.* London: Her Majesty's Stationery Office, 1965.

Rowe, Robert. *Adam Silver, 1765–1795.* London: Faber and Faber, 1965.

SILVERSMITHS

Barr, Elaine. *George Wickes, 1698–1761, Royal Goldsmith.* London: Studio Vista/Christie's, 1980.

Dickinson, H. W. *Matthew Boulton.* Cambridge: University Press for Babcock and Wilcox, 1936.

Goodison, Nicholas. *Ormolu: The Work of Matthew Boulton.* London: Phaidon Press, 1974.

Hayward, J. F. *The Courtauld Silver: An Introduction to the Work of the Courtauld Family of Goldsmiths.* London and New York: Sotheby Parke Bernet Publications, 1975.

Penzer, N. M. *Paul Storr, 1771–1844: Silversmith and Goldsmith.* London: B. T. Batsford, 1954. Reprint. London: Spring Books, 1971.

Phillips, P. A. S. *Paul de Lamerie: Citizen and Goldsmith of London.* London: Holland Press, 1968.

Royal Goldsmiths: The Garrard Heritage. London: Garrard Co., 1991.

Shure, David S. *Hester Bateman: Queen of English Silversmiths.* London: W. H. Allen, 1959.

Index of Silversmiths

Index of Objects

Beakers: double or fitted, 108; English, 50–51, 52–53, 54–55, 55–57, 59–60, 61–62, 108; Irish, 58; with stand, 58; travel, 52–53, 54–55, 55–57; in Virginia, 59–60, 109–110. *See also* Goblets

Bowls: handled, 4–5, 18–20, 21; miniature, 18–20, 44–45

Boxes. *See* Spice boxes

Canteens, travel, 52–53, 54–55, 55–57

Chalice, 10–11

Condiment jar lid, 55–57

Corkscrew, 55–57

Cups: American, 90; caudle, 43; as chalice, 10–11; covered, 1–2, 2–3, 3–4, 14–15, 28–29, 30–31, 33–34, 35, 36–37, 38, 39–40, 41–42, 90–92, 94–95, 96–98, 99–100, 106–107, 114–115, 116–117, 118–119, 119–121, 122–123, 123–124, 125–128; as duty dodger, 96–98; English, 1–2, 2–3, 6, 7–8, 9–10, 14–15, 16–17, 18–20, 27, 28–29, 30–32, 36–37, 38, 41–42, 42–43, 92–93, 94–95, 96–98, 99–100, 101–103, 106–107, 114–115, 116–117, 118–119, 119–121, 122–123, 123–124, 125–128; gourd-shaped, 14–15; handled, 1–2, 2–3, 3–4, 6, 14–15, 16–17, 18–20, 27, 28–29, 30–32, 33–34, 35, 36–37, 38, 39–40, 41–42, 42–43, 43–44, 44–45, 45–46, 90–92, 92–93, 94–95, 96–98, 99–100, 101–103, 104–105, 106–107, 114–115, 116–117, 118–119, 119–121, 122–123, 123–124, 125–128; Irish, 10–11, 35, 39–40, 45–46, 90–92, 101–103, 104–105; as military awards, 119–121, 125–128; miniature, 18–20, 44–45, 45–46; presentation, 16–17, 83, 106–107, 114–115, 116–117, 119–121, 123–124, 125–128; as racing trophies, 16–17, 83, 116–117, 123–124; Scottish, 33–34, 45–46, 76; spout, 36–37; thistle, 45–46, 76; U–body, 27, 28–29, 30–32, 33–34, 38; in Virginia, 99–100; wine, 7–8, 9–10, 10–11. *See also* Quaichs; Tumblers

Duty dodger, 97–98

Forks, 54–55, 55–56

Goblets, 62–63, 63–64, 64–65, 66–67, 68–69. *See also* Beakers

Graters, 55–57

Knives, 54–55, 55–56

Military awards, 119–121, 125–128

Miniatures: English, 18–20, 44–45; Irish, 45–46; Scottish, 45–46. *See also* Wine tasters

Mugs: American, 84–85, 112–113; Chinese, 112–113; covered, 70–71; English, 36–37, 44–45, 70–71, 72, 73, 74–75, 77–78, 79, 80–81, 82–83, 111, 112–113; Indian, 112–113; miniature, 44–45; in New York, 84–85; as racing trophies, 83; Scottish, 80–81; in Virginia, 84–85

Presentation vessels, 16–17, 83, 106–107, 114–115, 116–117, 119–121, 123–124, 125–128

Quaichs, 47–49. *See also* Cups

Racing trophies, 16–17, 83, 116–117, 123–124

Saucers, 12–13

Scoop, 55–57

Spice boxes, 52–53, 54–55, 57

Spoons, 54–55, 55–56

Stand, 58

Tankards: American, 88–89; English, 86–87, 109–110; Irish, 86–87; in New York, 88–89

Thistle cups, 45–46, 76

Treen, 25–26, 47–49

Tumblers: English, 22, 23–24, 25–26; nesting, 23–24; treen, 25–26. *See also* Cups

Vase, 125–128. *See also* Cups

Wine tasters, 17. *See also* Miniatures